GAUDEAMUS

A very liberal education, in two acts.

Suggested by
the *Ecclesiazusae* of Aristophanes

First published in 2006 by Oberon Books Ltd
Electronic edition published in 2013

Oberon Books Ltd
521 Caledonian Road, London N7 9RH
Tel: +44 (0) 20 7607 3637 / Fax: +44 (0) 20 7607 3629
e-mail: info@oberonbooks.com
www.oberonbooks.com

A catalogue record for this book is available from the British
Library.

PB ISBN: 978-1-84002-667-2
E ISBN: 978-1-78319-372-1

Front cover design: Dan Steward

eBook conversion by Replika Press PVT Ltd, India.

GAUDEAMUS

BY PETER MORRIS

Cast

Lynette Baker Chipo Chung
Helen West Kika Markham
Brad Kelly Travis Oliver

Creative Team

Director Michael Longhurst
Designer Patrick Burnier
Lighting Designer David Miller
Sound Designer Matt Downing
Associate Costume Designer Nell Knudsen
Assistant Director Alex Sutton
Production Manager Amy Matthews

For Arcola Theatre

Artistic Director Mehmet Ergen
Executive Producer Leyla Nazli

Special thanks: Anna Jones, Lloyd Trott, Anthony Shuster, Will Chambers, Davina Shah, Helen Eastman and all who have offered their support and talent to this production.

Again, for Joseph –

haec locutus, sustuli tunicam…

There is a God, and his name is Aristophanes.

– Heinrich Heine

I even take the position that sexual orgies eliminate social tensions and ought to be encouraged. But it is blindingly clear that judges have no greater capacity than the rest of us to decide what is moral.

– Justice Antonin Scalia, speaking at Harvard University on September 28, 2004

Characters

Lynette Baker
college-age (19) black girl. Confident, charismatic,
and breathtakingly intelligent.

Brad Kelly
college-age (20) white boy. Broad-shouldered,
good-looking, with a broad winning smile. He should
probably be blond, too – everything else about him
suggests the plodding earnest benevolence of
a Golden Retriever.

Professor Helen West
a grandmotherly (68) tenured Professor of Classics.
White-haired and bespectacled. Formidably learned,
with a bone-dry wit. She seems at once both prim and
utterly unshockable.

Time
The present.

Place
An experimental college in Vermont.

Act One

1. LYNETTE

Hello, strangers. Because that's what we are. Pretend it's the start of our freshman year. We're strangers.

And because we're strangers, what really interests me…is what you think you know already. About me. Before we've met.

Think of it like this. My favorite thing ever? Is the moment just before you kiss somebody for the first time. Before that, you're almost strangers. And afterward you're – something else. But in that one moment: you're leaning close, attracted, each of you catch your breath, and – you look deep into the other person's eyes, thinking: *right now, you and me, we could be anything…the possibilities are limitless, baby…you can be anything you wanna be…*

So you're nice people. Is that what you're thinking now? I could be anything?

Or are you thinking, 'Boy, she's *something!* She's so – articulate. 'Cause she's not some *ghetto stereotype,* y'know, unwed teenage mother, promiscuous *ho.* Gosh, you know what she could be? A lawyer, a CEO, or she could even be…*the next Oprah.*'

Well I hope you're *not* thinking that. 'Cause you're nice open-minded people, and an open mind is a terrible thing to waste. I'm gonna warn you straight off, I'm not *predictable.* So don't trade in that old stereotype for a new one…don't decide you already decided, okay? 'Cause that? Is still *Prejudice.*

Like a jury reaches a verdict in under a second, with no evidence, when the judgment's been made in advance. Prejudice. How so little information can govern so much. Of what we say, or think, or do. And even who we wanna kiss. But we're *strangers:* you don't even know my name yet.

Lynette Baker. Nice to meet you. And I'm a junior, majoring in – seriously, though, does anybody even *have* a major here? I'm doing some kinda poli-sci / philosophy / sociological mash-up, whatever classes I wanna take and you call it a major, but – that's how this place works. It's an *experimental college*. In Vermont.

So. Here's some political science for ya – the population of Vermont? Is 96.2 percent Caucasian. Whitest state in the union, don't mean snowfall. And here I am, in Vermont, and what would you say if I tell you: I feel *oppressed*.

Don't jump to conclusions, though – you're nice people, so *ask*: 'Lynette? What's oppressing you, girlfriend?' (Actually, *don't* say 'girlfriend'.) But don't be afraid to ask the question – is this some kinda – *racial* problem?

Yeah. It is. 'Cause my problem is Oprah. My problem is Oprah and Oprah Magazine and Oprah's Book Club. It's *The Cosby Show* and Johnny Cochrane and *Guess Who's Coming to Dinner?* It's that Star-Jones-and-Stella, Gettin-Her-Groove-Back, *Essence*-Magazine *bullshit*. Know what I'm talking about?

My problem's that I escape one stereotype only to get slapped with another. 'Cause look at me – I'm a straight-A student from a prep school, growing up in a 2-million dollar McMansion in Greenwich, Connecticut. Which *is* a ghetto, just…not the kind you might think.

In short, the problem is – my mom. Who isn't Oprah, but she might as well be. And look, I'm nineteen years old, and regardless of race, creed, color – like any woman my age I am oppressed by my mother. My mother, who lived through a revolution in the Sixties, and came out on the other side with – a B A from Barnard, a J D from Harvard, and a subscription to *Essence* Magazine. A six-figure salary and still she's got those glazed and greedy eyes like she just won the jackpot on some stupid-ass gameshow. 'Condoleeza, come on down… you're the next contestant on *The Rice Is White!*'

So she whisked me off in her Jaguar to attend those Jack and Jill meetings. And I grew up on Talented Tenth Avenue, right next to Alan and Alicia Keys. This is not some raisin in the sun, people. This is *sun-dried tomatoes*, Dean & Deluca, sixteen bucks a pound. Guess who's coming to dinner? Fuck that. Guess who's coming to *brunch*.

I mean, what happened to the Sixties? Equality, wasn't that the point? Doesn't matter if you're male or female, straight or gay, old or young, black or white – look at Angela Davis, middle-aged black Lesbian communist, she had John Lennon and Mick Jagger *both* writing songs about her.

So I'm still holding my breath for Angela's revolution, but my Mom? She's just waiting to exhale.

So. Is that social progress? Is that the true essence of equality?

No. That's just – *Essence* Magazine.

She holds up a copy of Essence Magazine.

You ever read this? When you're getting your hair straightened, maybe. Leaf through it sometime, and you'll understand my point: Condi Rice, meet Condé Nast. Upper-middle-class black folks can be just as fucking *dull* as the white variety. But me, I'm nineteen, I wanna have a life, I wanna have fun, I wanna – okay, let's be honest, I wanna have *sex*. Whereas my mom? Has *never had sex in her life*. There's only one Big O in mama's life, and that's Miss Winfrey.

So maybe my problem *isn't* racial. I mean, who cares my mom is black? Although she is, in fact, black in case you were wondering. I don't even think my mom cares. Ask her opinion of Racial Profiling, she'll tell you it's an *honor*. That time she was Profiled by *Essence* Magazine.

Lynette flips open the magazine, looks down, then looks up.

And okay, here…what I was looking for. This article, entitled: *Bring Me Home A Black Girl.* Written by the editor herself, Miss

Audrey Edwards. A true story of how she brainwashed her stepson *never* to date white women. *Bring Me Home A Black Girl.* Guess who's *not* coming to dinner. Audrey says...and I quote:

> '...When Black men marry out of the race, it not only further diminishes the number of brothers available to Black women, but it also undermines our very confidence as desirable women.'

Speak for yourself, sister. *Desirable?* Angela Davis made the Ten Most Wanted List, and she didn't even straighten her hair. Sweet black angel didn't even like *boys.*

But here's the statistics. In 1982, seventeen percent of teenagers said they'd dated somebody from a different race. Twenty years later, 2002, *fifty-seven percent* said they had. So it looks like progress, but...now I wanna tell you a story. Which should maybe tell you something.

There's this guy here at school. Brad. He's good-looking in an average way, I mean, he's like a likeable version of Ben Affleck. Or a straight version of Ben Affleck. And did I mention Brad is white? But you knew that. It's Vermont.

Now Brad's not the type to catch my eye, but – he's got a reputation. The kind of guy the girls around here think is *hot.* But that's not some kind of empirical fact. It's socially-determined. If only one girl can have him, all the others want him – what seventeenth-century economists called the Scarcity Theory of Value. Lord knows if all the girls could have him at once, they'd be bored in a week. As you may recall, that's what happened with Tickle Me Elmo dolls, back when I was a kid. Only this isn't Tickle Me Elmo. It's Fuck Me Brad.

Except here's what I noticed. The girls Brad dates? They're *identical.* Like he walks down the hallway of life, and the wallpaper's got this endlessly-repeating pattern of blonde hair and open vaginas. Mean, they are identical as wallpaper, they're *all the same.* And that's not prejudice, 'cause I know them, he dated my freshman roommate Jamie – although, for the purposes of brevity, I'll make the prejudicial comment about these girls and say: you know the type.

You know the type and if it helps, at the prep school I attended, we useta call them 'lacrosse-titutes'.

Okay, so spring term last year, we're all at some afterparty for this *a cappella* singing group – which is bullshit, nobody actually likes *a cappella* singing, they just go to the party 'cause they got free beer. And I'm talking with a bunch of my friends, and Brad's there too. And I knew Jamie had just dumped him a few days before, for hooking up with some other girl. But when Jamie told me this, crying, I didn't rush to judgment. 'Cause really, these girls do look identical, maybe Brad made an honest mistake.

So I'm standing there looking at Brad. He's drunk. He's sulky. He's practically licking his nuts like an injured tomcat. Why? 'Cause he came to this party for one reason only – to find some friend of Jamie's, and fuck her to piss Jamie off. But it's getting late, and it's clear that Brad just doesn't wanna be there.

And I'm looking at Brad, but he doesn't look at me. Not till I clear my throat and say, 'Hey, all, think I'm gonna head back to the dorm.'

And since Brad has got all the fake chivalry of a genuine horndog, he says: 'Hey, I'll walk you back, Lynette.' Not like there's any danger on this campus if I walk alone. He just wants an excuse to get outta there. And I'm the excuse.

So I'm walking with Brad, and it's – well, it's slightly awkward. He's not saying a thing. So I say, 'Heard you broke up with Jamie.'

Brad says, 'Yeah.'

And I said, 'And who was it before her?'

He's like, 'What?'

And I said, 'Who'd you date before Jamie?'

And he says, 'Prolly Becky Haslanger, or – you mean *dated* dated, or hooked up?'

And I say, 'Does it *matter,* Brad? They all look the same.'

And he's like, 'Yeah, well, guess I have a type.'

And I say, '*Stereo*type is more like it.'

And *of course* he instantly gets terrified. He says, 'Wha…what's that supposed to mean?'

So I pounce.

I say, 'Brad…you ever date a black girl?'

(You can see, I'm giving him more attitude now. 'Cause if those stereotypes *are* still bouncing around out there, you better believe I'm gonna use 'em to my advantage.)

And Brad says no, so I say: 'Isn't that a little racist?'

And Brad's like, 'I'm not *racist*! I've just…never dated a black girl.'

And I say, '*Mm-hmm.* Don't get defensive, Brad. But that proves it.'

And he says, 'Look, it's not – racism, it's more like – like not having the opportunity?'

And I say, '*Exactly.* You're not an equal-opportunity horndog.'

And he says, 'Come on! Don't say that!'

And I put my hand on my hip and say, 'Brad, you walkin through a diverse world and you always pick the same thing. You're like a little boy looking at all those thirty-one flavors in Baskin Robbins and you always pick *vanilla.* If that's not racist, I don't know what is.'

And he's like, 'So, what, I've got racist taste?'

And I say, 'Well, you just admitted to me you ain't never tasted Brown Sugar before.'

Do you *see* the game I was playing? I swear to god I was in *ecstasy*. 'Cause

Brad looks at me and I can tell – somewhere inside that thick lacrosse-playing skull, somewhere in there, the hamster starts runnin on the wheel, and the little light goes on, and he says, 'Lynette, uh…are you saying something?'

We're outside my dorm. And I say: 'Brad. I'm saying you a *racist.*'

And suddenly he's – well, it's like he's looking at me for the first time. Looking into my eyes. And he says, 'So, uh, how can I prove to you that I'm not?'

And I unlock that door so fast, grab his hand and we run up the stairs and into my room, and I throw a scarf over the desk lamp, I shove him backwards onto the bed, I straddle him, then I look down into his eyes and he's *caught.* So just to *amuse* myself – just to be *cruel* – I lean in real close and I say: 'Honey, you want me to put on a *slow jam* or you just want some *gospel music?*'

Then I reach over to press play on the stereo, and praise the lawd we got Sweet Honey in the Rock and I look down at Brad…then I pin him and mount him like a butterfly.

Triumph.

Well…yes and no. Like I said, the *truly* sexy part happens before the first kiss. And frankly, Brad was a lousy lay. It just proved his popularity had nothing to do with merit. Tickle Me Elmo.

But here's the point… Afterwards, after the clean-up and the small talk, after he awkwardly kisses me on the top of the head, says 'See you around, 'kay?' – and goes… I'm just sitting there, alone. *Smiling.*

Until I think: What the fuck? Am I actually proud of myself?

Cause I *was* proud, a little bit, thinking how *furious* my mom
would be, not to mention the editor of *Essence* Magazine.
But also I'm thinking: well, guess I'm in their club now,
Jamie, and Becky and all the lacrosse-titutes. Then it hits
me…Why should I be proud of *that*? I mean, Brad was
genuinely mediocre – I woulda done better with a cucumber,
sexually *and* conversationally – but I'm sitting on the bed and
grinning, like I just got crowned the winner of this year's Miss
Cegenation Pageant? Why? And – literally – what the fuck.

And at that moment – and sorry, I know, this is *such* an
undergraduate thing to say – at that moment, what pops into
my mind is the debate over reparations for slavery.

'Cause what I'm thinking…maybe you could say what I did
to Brad's like reparations. He's forced to pay for something he
didn't do. But I forced him. Seriously. He didn't have a choice.
He can't say no. Which means – omigod, it was *date rape?* That
freaks me out. I just date-raped a white fratboy.

Now I'm all nervous, and I think: who can I call? I can't call
Jamie, because – well, date-rape or not, I just slept with her ex.
She'd *kill* me. I'm not even thinking, but somehow I dial the
numbers and – I call my mom.

And she says 'What's the matter? Are you having a problem,
Lynette?'

And I say 'Not really. Sorta. It's a boy.'

She says 'Are you dating him?'

I say 'No, nothing like that. I don't think he's interested, but
the problem is – '

And *instantly* she interrupts and says 'He's white, isn't he.' Just
like that. 'He's white, isn't he.' Do you believe that?

I just say, 'Where the fuck did that come from?'

And she laughs and says, 'Lynette, mothers *always* know.
Don't act like I just told you to sue him for discrimination.
Although…if you want to?'

And I shout down the phone at her, 'You're as racist as
everybody else! As a matter of fact, I just *date-raped a white boy*.
But don't worry, mom. I'll bring you home a black girl. I'll
become a lesbian like Angela Davis, if you even *remember* her.'

And Mom says, 'I remember the hairstyle. And didn't she end
up in prison?' At which point I hang up the phone.

Because honestly. My generation, me, Brad, anybody my
age – all we want is a way for this shit *not to matter* anymore.
We want something…different, and new, and sexy. We want
– *Equality*.

If Equality means, you can look into *anyone's* eyes, and say:
Baby, you and me, we could be anything. And that's sexy. Isn't it?
Equality's sexy.

But me and Brad? It was – a joke, or poetic justice, and I'm
definitely not proud of it, and I'm pretty sure now it wasn't
date rape but anyway it's his word against mine. But the
weirdest thing of all – is that it wasn't sexy. I'm not his type,
he's not mine. But what's the difference between that, and
– and discrimination? 'Cause we'll never have Equality, unless –

Unless we are all Completely *Un*-Discriminating. Totally
Indiscriminate. About who we wanna…kiss. You know what
I'm saying? Yeah, I think you do.

So. You're nice open-minded people, right? What are you
thinking now?

'Um, she *is* articulate but – wow, seriously, is she *also* a
promiscuous ho?'

Well, I did warn you: I'm not predictable. But soon enough
you'll see what I've got planned. But first – look deep into my
eyes, all of you. Right now, before we start.

'Cause if you look in my eyes you *know* this ain't *Guess Who's Coming To Dinner?*

Look in my eyes and all we're gonna be saying, is… *Baby… Guess Who's Coming…*

2. BRAD

Dude.

Okay, this is some crazy shit, so I gotta –

This. Is an Experimental College, right? Which, practically speaking, I don't even really know what that means, I mean, who's experimenting on who, man?

And ordinarily it boils down to nothing. It means that we can make up our own majors – like there's this Goth Chick majoring in Death Studies? – and it means you can take everything pass-fail, and it means only 26 credits to graduate, which means –

Well, put it this way. I applied here 'cause this guy I know said those New England Experimental Colleges? It isn't college. It's *sex camp*.

And fuckit, my dad'll totally get me into law school, doesn't matter where I go to undergrad, I mean, fuckin' University of Aruba, 'cause his firm'll hire me after, so – why not go to sex camp for 4 years? Dad can afford it, and hey, it even sounds intellectual to him. Like I come home for Thanksgiving and tell him I'm taking 'Depictions of the Other in Contemporary Cinema,' y'know, watch *Independence Day* and pretend it's secretly about Mexican immigrants. Or else 'American Folklore,' the urban legends class – and Dad thinks I'm really really deep. He thinks that's what college *is* these days. He's got *no clue* that I'm here to, like – Ski, and Fuck.

Although in all honesty, speaking about my, uh, higher education, I must say...I ski a lot less than I expected.

But getting laid? *Dude.* Much as you'd think. But I won't say much as I *want* because, well... who gets that? I know they say 'sexual appetite' like it's an *appetite*, like: eat one piece of that pie and you'll feel full. But it's not that kind of appetite, is it? I mean what's the limit?

But I'm getting to that.

'Cause look. It ain't *easy.* I mean, these days we are beyond the old Catholic girl situation Billy Joel useta sing about, where they *never* give it up. But you are not just wading knee-deep in an acre of pussy either. All I mean is: even at a place like this, it's still an arm-wrestling match. You gotta *work.*

Like this one girl I was seeing, sorta, I'm tryin to talk her into having, y'know, anal sex. You know the drill. I gave her the old line about nerve endings, I promised I would offer her, uh, clitoral stimulation the whole time I was up there, I promised I would take it gentle and – well, I said a lotta stuff, I mean, it's *salesmanship,* right? Go slow and smooth and wear 'em down, and *bang.* Arm-wrestling.

So anyway, I talk her into it, Jamie, her name was Jamie, and I – well, I'm not into hurting her but let's be honest: it's buttfucking. So I get her on all fours and, well, she was pretty cute but bein like that made her tits hang down and look kinda – look, I know how this sounds here but at least I'm being honest – they were great tits but kinda stretchmarky, and she...well, you always think a girl like that is gonna look – like thin, and hot, with those hot bony hips, but when she's naked she looks like – well, like everybody else.

But I'm into it, and I'm givin it to her, hard, and I'm, like, *focused,* and – I guess I was quiet. 'Cause she says, 'Brad, *say* something' and I think, uh-oh. So I think fast and I say 'Mmm, yeah, Jamie, it's like I'm a bottle of wine and I'm pouring myself all over you but you don't get wet' and she says 'Why not?' She actually asks me, and I just say 'Cause I'm…a very dry white wine.' Really smooth, hunh? But then she says 'No, say something else' and I'm like, what? And she's like: 'I wanna know you *empathize* with me.'

So I said, yeah I do, Jamie, I really really do, till I shoot my wad, then I lay down next to her, and – I *cuddle*. 'Cause I may not learn much at this place, but I did learn *that* trick.

And it's only later that I think to myself: fuck does *that* mean? *Empathize*?

And I think, Welp, only at an Experimental School.

But now, and this is the crazy shit I mentioned, now I know what Experimental School *means*. Means, the student body's in charge. The student senate makes the rules, and what they say goes for *everyone*, even faculty. And if all this sounds like a Sixties kinda thing, you know, like a four-in-the-morning let's-take-another-hit-of-acid-and-play-that-Jefferson-Starship-L.P.-backwards thing, I should also tell you that normally, nothing results from this. The student senate is mainly freaks who couldn't organize a peanut butter and jelly sandwich. Let alone, like, a totally – radical idea. Until now.

And even now, it's not the senate that came up with the idea. It's one person.

It's Lynette.

I mean, I know Lynette.

I, uh, well. I fucked Lynette.

I mean it was fine, she came on pretty strong one night and why not, I mean, pretty fuckin obnoxious to turn a girl down for sex. And it was fine, not my best, not my worst, and afterward, well – it didn't become awkward because she's not the kind of girl I actually socialize with, so it turned into more of a –

'Kay, you know when you meet all those people at freshman orien – fresh*person* – orientation, and you make small talk with, like, all these people you're meeting blind till you figure out: most of them you have nothing in common with. So when you walk past 'em in the Quad two years later you're like – *what?* Do I pretend we're total strangers? Or do I say hi?

I mean, I'm not the only person who finds this awkward, am I? 'Cause it's the opposite of, well, the *real* world – where all you ever meet is people with your own interests and background and you *wanna* make small talk 'cause – 'cause that's networking. But this is…the opposite. Like trying not to rub it in that you have nothing in common with this person. Except this, like, narrow strip of pavement across the Quad.

Which is where I met Lynette this afternoon.

And she's got this huge folder, and she's, like, sashaying straight at me and I'm thinking, Yokay, gotta say hi to this one, 'cause I boned her…But before I open my mouth, she says to me: 'Brad. Just the man I wanna see.'

And she sounds just like she did that night when she's, like, begging me to fuck her. And I'm thinking: Jesus Christ. Broad daylight, dead sober, six months later middle of the Quad and she's moist for a rematch *now?*

But y'know, I'm *polite.* So I say 'Hey Lynette. What kin I do you for?'

And she says, 'I'm on my way to the senate. Can you sign this?' And holds out this form.

And I know what this school is like, but Dad would *shit* if he found out I signed some Howard Dean thing. Seriously. So I'm like, 'What is it?'

And she snaps, 'I've got time to get a signature, Brad, not to *explain.* Unless you wanna walk.'

And the way she says it makes me think: what the fuck, no classes, too early for beer, but – she's walking fast and I'm just about keeping up, so I gotta ask, 'Uh, Lynette, what's this all about?'

And she says, '*Discrimination.* New rules. I want the student senate to pass.'

And I'm like, 'There's no rules for that already?'

And she's like, 'This is different. It's like an Experiment. I'm saying – '

Then she stops, and looks at me, and smiles. And she says: 'Put it this way, Brad. Has anyone ever turned you down for sex?'

And I'm like, 'Well, honestly? Not lately.'

And she says, 'Then you're asking the wrong people.'

And I'm a little miffed 'cause what does *that* mean? So I say, 'What does *that* mean?'

And she just says: 'If you never get turned down, you're only asking one kind of person to fill the job. And maybe that's *discrimination.*'

And I have *no clue* why she's got this chip on her shoulder, so I'm like, 'Well, (A) I can't exactly fuck the girls who *do* turn me down, if there were any, because that is *date rape,* I think, and (B) not to get personal, Lynette? but I did fuck *you* which does indicate some concern for, uh, diversity.'

And she just says, 'Look, I'm not attacking you, Brad. I'm trying to say: what if you lived in a world where nobody says no? Where nobody turns anyone down for sex.'

And I and I – I just laugh and say, 'Bring it on, girlfriend!'

And she looks at me and says, 'Don't condescend to me, you fucking mouthbreather. Just just come to the senate, vote yes to the motion, I'll fucking bring it on. And vice versa.'

So we go into the student center and she gives that huge folder to this secretary dude, who's, I mean, sweet Jesus, must really need to pad his resumé. And the senate's called to order, then Mister Secretary clears his throat and says: 'There's a motion? For structural and constitutional change to school regulations.' He says that like he's gonna fudge his undies (or just did). 'Cause apparently this is something heavy. And they call up Lynette to explain.

Now I'm prolly the wrong person to be telling this story because even though I was one of the few eyewitnesses there – and this'll go down in history, I promise, but uh. I'm not real good at taking stuff in when I hear it? I'm a visual learner. But when Lynette starts talking – fuck, man, the world just *moves*, the world turns upside *down*. But I'm, uh, gonna have to paraphrase, pretty much.

She gets up, starts by saying: You'll agree we're all united against prejudice – and everybody nods, they're thinking, mm-hmm, oh yes, we listen to Moby of course we agree – then she says: But how can we *eradicate* it? Look at this school. We're diverse, we're multicultural...and it doesn't teach us anything but tolerance. And tolerance *sucks*. People tolerate what they *don't like*. Tolerance is a result of prejudice, so it can't help destroy it. So I'd like to propose a radical...Experiment. Then she reads it.

And basically it says: *nobody's allowed to turn another person down for sex.*

Like, that's the gist.

And the room's, like, totally silent.

And Mister Secretary's like: (*BRAD just lets his jaw hang open.*)

And Lynette says: It's not enough to say: don't judge a book by its cover. We need to make it law. That you can *only* judge a book *between* the covers. And the entire student body is your required reading. Questions?

And there's like this total uproar 'cause – 'cause holy shit, *think* about it – and the chairm – chairperson, he asks her – You know this contradicts these other rules we have, like about sexual harassment and date rape? And Lynette says, We always wanted to make those things obsolete: now we can. And somebody else says, Can we still *date?* Sure, she says, but all relationships must be open relationships by law. So you'd only stay together if it's true love, right?

So now *I* raise my hand and I say, uh, yeah, can a college even *do* this? And Lynette smiles and says if fuckin Bob Jones University *bans* interracial dating 'cause they're a private institution, who's gonna tell us we can't mandate this? (Seriously, she's winning us over.)

Then this goth chick, the Death Studies major, gets up. And she is *so* not a happy camper, mean, even less than usual. And she says, 'Don't you think there's more pressing political concerns in the world than – than *this?*'

And Lynette says: 'Look at the world. You and I both see the same problems: inequality, destruction, bigotry, war. You're telling me it's not the profoundest statement we can make, to commit ourselves to perfect equality and pleasure? You don't think that sends a message to the world?'

So the chair guy says, Well, are you aware this requires a quorum of the student body – some shit like that – which is seven hundred votes? And she says, Mr Chairperson, I've submitted over eight hundred proxy votes. I move we proceed to voting.

And – it passed.

And suddenly everybody's talking, running to get cellphone reception – Lynette's being slapped on the back by the senate's faculty adviser, Professor Gergen, who's this ex-hippie hits on all the girls anyway, only now it's like his civic duty – and there's the Goth Chick, asking the chairman if *he* thinks this would truly help the anti-globalization campaign – and the secretary dude's just typing it all up, poor sad fucker. But it's clear everybody knows: this is history in the making. And, well, lemme be honest: at that moment, I kinda got a chub-on.

So hey. Sex camp. Literally. I mean, the possibilities are Fuckin Limitless. And, as Lynette would say: vice –

Fuck.

Y'know, something just occurred to me.

If the rules are nobody can say no to me, then the rules are that I can't say no to, uh – anybody. At all. Which is –

Which is fine. I guess. It's diversity, balances out, and overall it's like – hey, I'm not a magnet for the ugly chicks or anything, and, uh – if it's seriously a radical Equality Experiment, then it all boils down to one basic important principle, right?

I can fuck anybody I want.

Within the school community, that is.

But it does occur to me that…I know I said a sexual appetite isn't like – but – *still.*

I only have one *dick,* dude.

    Pause, then BRAD grins.

Good thing there's ten inches of it, huh? Enough to go around.

3. HELEN

Good afternoon, ladies and gentlemen, and – heavens. What a turnout. Are you sure you all have the right class? I'm Professor West, Humanities 360-A: 'Rational and Irrational in Ancient Greece and Rome.'

Right. Well. Those who have studied with me before will know: I conduct this course on a modified Oxbridge-tutorial basis. Two abridged lectures per week, then an individual session, in my office, and…what am I forgetting? Oh, yes. Sign-up sheets for these sessions are posted by the doors. Please write your names, and you musn't be offended if I forget them – as I like to say, I'm up to the Z in Alzheimer's.

Also: though I may quote Greek and Latin in my lectures, I'll try to provide loose translations as we go. But should you have further questions regarding the meaning, please ask one your fellows who is proficient in these tongues. Edward, for example – hello, Edward – has the benefit (if that's the word) of a Jesuit secondary education. And if anyone else here –

And I *am* sorry, but I must inquire: Is anyone in this *throng* actually taking my class? Come now. My dears: to see such a large turnout for an upper-level classics seminar…no-one could be more surprised than I. Surprised, but – tickled pink. Young people often seem to have a prejudice against the classics these days. You think, without any evidence, that they're irrelevant. Plato, Aristophanes, Catullus…me. You think we're dry as dust, that our fountain of knowledge just – tapped out, long ago, like a frathouse keg. But darlings? I can tell you. That's a stereotype. The fountain's still flowing, but beware. As you may have heard:

A little learning is a dangerous thing:

Drink deep, or taste not the Pierian spring.

So. You have your reasons for coming here today, but I'm here to offer you a drink. A little learning. Think of it as a fountain, and – let's get wet. Shall we?

HELEN speaks the following text in Greek as she writes it on the chalkboard.

Τὰ μέγιστα τῶν ἀγαθῶν ἡμῖν γίγνεται διὰ μανίας

That. Is Socrates speaking. In Plato's dialogue, called the *Phaedrus*. Let me translate:

Τὰ μέγιστα – the greatest

τῶν ἀγαθῶν – of good things, or, a bit more fancifully yet with greater accuracy *of blessings,*

ἡμῖν γίγνεται – to us is born, comes to us

διὰ μανίας – by way of mania. Through *madness.*

The greatest of blessings comes to us through madness.

Now if you read further in the *Phaedrus* – and I'm sure there's some of you who still do that, read – every year there's one or two – if you read further you'll notice. One type of madness Plato describes is – *sex.* The madness of Eros. Sex-madness. Crazy sex. Why? Because it's not entirely rational, is it? You'd know better than I, sex isn't something that we can be totally rational about. That's why Eros, or Cupid, is frequently depicted with a blindfold. Love is *blind.* An impulse possesses you, like a demon – and that's the word Plato uses, actually. Δαίμων or – demon. A hot burning passion that possesses your soul completely. Some of you may have first-hand experience of this, which you may feel free to recollect.

However. Plato doesn't see sex as totally and utterly nutty. He *also* thinks it can provide the energy to drive the soul forward, in search of more…lasting satisfactions. Eros can lead us toward permance, perfection, toward an *ideal* – a Platonic ideal. This is where we get the slightly inaccurate modern notion of Platonic Love, right? We use it to mean…just holding hands. But in truth, Platonic love is not celibacy *per se*, but rather a long slow progress, over many years, in which gradually you learn, you grow, you acquire wisdom, and you eventually discover that you have become so wise that you don't even need to attract any students. You can just – sit in an empty classroom, and look at them from the window. And that's *progress*. Sex begets love, love begets – education, and we all climb higher toward something that transcends the merely physical things of this world: the dust and dirt, the earth, the body, the grave. Because for Plato sex is not just about sex. It's about – the desire for perfection. Approaching an *ideal*.

Did I just hear a yawn? I thought so. My dears, let's be frank. You're not here to learn from me, are you? Which is a pity, because I've been at this college for many years, trying to learn from you. This is – this is a *sit-in*. You are all here in this classroom, to see if I will sign this form.

She holds up the form.

This…Platonic form. Because you passed a law which says that, by the end of my first class, I must either sign this, or leave the college, exiled from the Garden of Eden with a kaftan of figleaves, and – leaving all of you behind, still naked, as you frolic beneath the Tree of Knowledge, leaving the fruit unplucked.

My, my, my. What can I say? I'm sixty-eight, and I remember 'sixty-eight. Vaguely. I was rather distracted by my work on the grammatical peculiarities of the *Oedipus Coloneus* at the time, so I didn't get out much. But is that what this is? Revolution? The topsy-turvy logic of Utopia, where suddenly the mind is controlled by the body, the *student* body, and the lunatic called sex is running the asylum? It's Cloud Cuckoo Land, as Aristophanes calls it. You kids pass a law and suddenly a square's a circle, day is night, and black is – beautiful. Well, why not. Why not indeed. Because I'd like you to give me the benefit of the doubt. Whatever you may have heard about Classics professors, I'm not some reactionary.

Don't be fooled by appearances. Not every little old lady with a copy of Plato's *Republic* is Allan Bloom. If indeed any of you have heard of Allan Bloom. Or Plato's *Republic,* for that matter.

The point is – I'm hip to your drift, I'm down with your multi-culty vibe. In fact, I've been there before you, long before, two millennia before – with Catullus, a sex-crazed youngster like yourselves, who made *this* political statement. To Julius Caesar, the man who would be Emperor, Catullus said:

> Nil nimium studeo, Caesar, tibi velle placere,
> nec scire utrum sis albus an ater homo.

Yes, *homo,* but don't giggle. Catullus says: *frankly, Caesar, I couldn't give a damn if you're black or white, and I'm not gonna kiss your ass either.* (Loose translation.) So if that's the song you're dancing to nowadays, how very *retro* – they knew the tune way back in the first century BC, my dears. And it still makes me tap my toes, if not swing my hips. Why? Because I'm a *teacher,* just like Socrates himself. I'm not young myself, not anymore, not *chronologically,* but I have spent decades in the company of young people like yourselves, one or two of them a year, on average, but – I am interested in youth,and in you. Like Socrates with Alcibiades, I want to know what you young people are thinking. Or sometimes whether you are thinking. But I do not care about your gender, your sexual orientation, or the color of your skin. These days, I can't even tell what you look like unless I wear my bifocals, frankly.

But I did put on my specs to read *this.* And I'm fascinated. Because it's not about black white straight gay girl boy, it's not the old PC identity politics at all, is it? That would be impossible, since I have it on good authority that one *loses* one's identity in the sex act. Ecstasy? From the Greek: ἔκστασις. I suppose it's all Greek to me, but to the Ancient Greeks, ecstasy meant…feeling your soul leap out of your body. Losing your identitity. And why not? I have no objections. At my age, identity can feel at times like – a corset,

a straightjacket, that you've been wearing for years, never
– cutting loose, breathing free –

So. If I read this correctly, then honestly, I'm intrigued.
Because this immodest proposal does indeed seem rational.
Reasonable. Sane. Honestly, it does. That's not the problem
with it. And that's not why I worry your experiment might be
doomed to failure.

The problem is that sex is *not* so rational. Is it? Honestly, I'm
asking the question. Is sex *rational*? Plato says no, Catullus says
no, Aristophanes says *fuck* no – that's a literal translation – but
the law says I can't say no.

So what? If I'm the teacher, I must approach this question like
Socrates. I confess my perfect ignorance. So there's no reason
whatsoever to assume that I'll be proved right, my dears. Let
us eat, drink and be merry. Let copulation thrive. I'm with you
all the way, I know I said this experiment will fail, but I'm not
Cassandra. I'm not even Allan Bloom. I'm willing to admit I
don't know *anything*. And *sex*? Sex! What do I know about sex?
If I haven't made it perfectly clear, I'm a sixty-eight year old
virgin!

So I'll sign your form. Because…what do I have to lose?
Besides (I might decorously add) the obvious.

> *HELEN signs the form. She is breathing heavily and looks
> flushed.*

There you go. I give my consent to the law. Stipulating that
anyone at this college, student or teacher, anyone may ask for,
and be granted, whatsoever carnal gratification he, or she, may
desire. See. I signed it.

Where are you going?

Oh. Well. If that's all you kids wanted was a big John
Hancock, then fine. Be on your way. You don't want what I
have to offer. I know that. Next week, there will only be four
of you, or one, or none. I know *that* old tune. Latin and Greek,

love'em and leave'em. Ave atque Vale, then toot-toot-tootsie goodbye –

Unless perhaps –

Yes. Before you go? Your assignment for the coming week.

Whether you're taking this seminar or not – and I understand that most of you are not, but do pay attention nonetheless. I want you all to please sign up on the sheets I've posted by the exit? For a one-hour session. Where each of you, black or white, straight or gay, male or female, honestly I don't care –

Each of you will furnish me with *cunnilingus*.

And if you have any difficulty with that Latin term, please ask one of your fellows.

4. LYNETTE

It's midterms and it's looking like a revolution, a successful revolution, like the American or the Sexual revolution, my God you should *see* it. Although I don't know how you'd see it, because – this revolution will *not* be televised, brother. Like if Malcolm was rated triple-X. Like if Doctor King gave us sexual healing. I have a dream, too – and it's wet. *Everybody's* getting laid.

Everybody but me, that is. I'm too busy, working to get the SSS up and running. That's Student Sexual Services. But once we get this infrastructure in place – with all the request forms that need to be processed, the procedural stuff, so you can file a grievance if you get stood up – once it's *automated*, I'll start having fun. Let's just hope that the state will wither away before all the boys do. Till then, I'm up to my eyes in paperwork. Which is *not* what I was expecting.

Like: I wanted a Blue Movie, and all I get is – Red Tape.

Although let me be clear. I *could* fill out one of these forms, if I wanted to. Put in a request for Brad, see if he's learned anything. But you know what? I'd rather wait for Brad to request me. 'Cause pleasure's not the point: equality is.

And long as I'm working late, least I've got time to think. About how new and different and *perfect* this campus feels now. Although it's hard to put your finger on it – although Lord knows people are putting their fingers on a lotta things, but –

Okay, what I think? This'll sound paradoxical, but – I'll explain. One of my best friends here? Is Eddie. Edward. Eddie's a Humanities major and he's – well – okay, add it up. 'Cause it's –

As she says these, she touches her shirt, her thighs, her belt-buckle, navel, then ears.

Abercrombie, Abercrombie, 2eXist, navel-pierce, and – oh yeah, Belle & Sebastian on the iPod. Mm-hmm? That's right. When you see me with Eddie you just know we are part of the historic alliance between faggots and black girls with attitude. But freshman year, Eddie didn't actually come out right away, which, *really*. This place? Not hard to do. I mean, I'd ask (politely) and he'd say, 'I don't really know what I am yet.'

Then he did the math. And he's ready to take those first mincing steps. So he asks me, would I go clubbing with him, down in Boston? Some underage gay club he's heard about, all 18-to-21 year old faggots, called *Buzz* or *Fierce* or some lame name that's like catnip for the junior butt-pirate crowd. Anyway, I say yes, figuring it'll be fine, but when we walked into the place – my heart just sank.

'Cause I look around and…it's like all the worst things about being a thirteen-year-old girl. It's all Britney Spears and body-glitter, bitchery and bulimia and *boys boys boys*. Who's got the bluest eyes, the bubbliest butt. Until – I felt something. Almost like what I'm feeling here, now, on campus. A perfect mix, of – youth, and the first dizzy headrush of liberation, and somehow finding yourself among equals, in a place that's – safe. And that's what makes it perfect: feeling *safe*.

'Cause look, before I went to Boston with Eddie, I'd been to plenty of clubs, straight clubs. And when you're a woman on a crowded dancefloor, think how you feel those eyes, predatory, masculine, sizing you up with that macho gaze. And obviously the gays don't give a girl the gaze. But they don't ignore you either. 'Cause they know that, for a girl, sometimes it's even worse to *not* feel those eyes...to feel invisible. And that night with Eddie I'm being *worshipped*, surrounded on all sides, like Diana Ross in *The Wiz*, surrounded on the dancefloor by a whole lollipop guild of fidgety little apprentice faggots, as we're all dancing to the world's longest shittiest remix of *Slave 4 U* by Britney Spears.

And I thought to myself, this is *almost* perfect. Just one problem. Well, Britney, yeah that's a problem – but one *big* problem. I have zero chance of getting laid in a gay club.

But here and now on this campus? Problem solved. Nobody feels violated, nobody feels invisible, and everybody's fucking. Trust me. They are. I know they've been fucking for the same reason that I haven't been – because I'm the one processes the paperwork. But I'm not complaining. 'Cause Equality? It's an ideal. Which means: you wanna live up to the ideal, you better work it, girl. And you make sacrifices. You *have* to.

Like...

'Kay, first thing we did to set up SSS was file all the signed consent forms, says you know the rules. And you don't sign, you're outta here. So I'm reviewing all the names, faculty, students, to make sure there's no honeychild left behind. And I find – just one. Who didn't sign, but didn't drop out either. Slipped through the cracks, so to speak. And it's...Josh Rosenberg.

Now I know Josh. Sometimes we end up sitting together in the dining hall. 'Cause Josh always sits alone, and I refuse to sit at that one lonely table where every other black student is sitting, by choice. Then we have dinner, purely to argue with each other. We can't help it.

'Cause you can probably guess from the name…Josh Rosenberg? Is a *Libertarian*.

And in case you don't know what that is? Well. An undergrad Libertarian is a boy, *always* a boy, usually got nice Democrat parents he's trying to piss off. And he arrives at college with only two books in his suitcase: a well-thumbed copy of *Bartlett's Familiar Quotations,* and a paperback of *The Fountainhead* with all the pages spooged together.

I know Josh pretty well and honestly – I hate him. 'Cause yo? Josh? It's *Vermont.* Howard Dean, Civil Unions, Bernie Sanders, Ben and Jerry's? We're *Socialists*, shithead. Libertarians thatta way: New Hampshire. Live free or die. Then fuck off *and* die. At Dartmouth.

But Josh is the only person who hasn't signed the form, so – I have to deal with him. So I go to his dormroom. The door is locked (of course). So I open it with a passkey, to see geeky Josh, in his boxers, reading *The Virtue of Selfishness* by Ayn Rand through his coke-bottle glasses. I'd never seem him undressed – he's skinny but – kinda cute.

And he looks up and says, 'Who said you could come in?'

And I say, 'Business call, Josh.'

And he says, 'Oh. So not a booty call then.'

And I say, 'You want booty, here's your duty.' And I hold out the form, and a pen.

And he says, 'Look. It's a matter of principle. Sure I'll fuck a girl if she asks for it, but I'm not signing some – some *social contract*.'

And I say, 'Josh? You wanna get laid, you sign. We got laws.'

And he looks up at me with this fucking *smug* – I can't believe this, he actually looks me in the eye, and smirks, and says: 'Look, lady. Keep *your* laws off *my* body.'

Oh and *now* I'm pissed. 'Cause it's a matter of principle for me too. And I can respect diversity of opinon, but – shouldn't a college keep *stupid* people out? That's how I feel about Libertarians. The same way Libertarians feel about black students, pretty much.

But I bite my tongue and I say, politely, 'Josh, as a Libertarian, you believe in total freedom. Don't you believe in Free Love?'

And he says 'Free Love? Fuck that. That just gives chicks like you a Free Lunch.'

And I look at him and say 'Josh honey, you forgetting I *know* you? You couldn't get your sorry ass laid on *J-Date*. In fact, you couldn't get laid in *prison*. So don't tell *me* that you don't benefit from Free Love.'

And Josh says, 'Whoa! Scuuuuse me, *Hillary*. But this is *Fucking Welfare,* and vice versa. Big government, bureaucracy…the road to serfdom, babe. If that's Free Love, just gimme Free Association. Gimme *Free Trade.*'

And I say, '*Love* isn't *globalized economics* Josh. It's not some – transaction.'

And he says, 'Sure it is. Back where you come from, Lynette? Didn't the hos trade handjobs for crack?'

And I say, 'Oh what, and you can get it for me wholesale? Oh Lawdy me, I specs things sho' must be different back in *Hymietown.*'

And we're staring at each other, total fuming ideological deadlock, steam coming out our nostrils, till I see that – there – poking out of his boxers, he has got a hard-on as thick and long as *Atlas Shrugged*. And I realize instantly that, omigod,

principles shminciples, I am – *so* – *turned* – *ON*, and we just
– *hit it*, animals, pouncing, rutting, oh my holy Jesus fuck…

That was sex.

Sparks were flying, it's like some – *love drug*, like I gave him
an afro-centro-disiac and while he slips me a Fiddler on the
Roofie, and we're out of our minds and *flying* on Malcolm
X-Stasy and Irving Kristol Meth, and suddenly we know we're
gonna make music. We're gonna make the Beastie Boy with
two backs, gonna dance the horizontal hava-na-gila, gonna
wrap ourselves in that white sheet like we're tryin to integrate
the Klan. It's like the Last Tango in Crown Heights. We're
making *music,* making *love,* honestly truly we are making…
Whoopi…Goldberg.

And the whole time I was thinking, oh, yes, this is the true
meaning of diversity.

So we're lying there, drenched in sweat, speechless, spent, and
I'm just gently trailing my fingernails across his hairy back,
and I whisper to him, 'So Josh? *Now* you gonna sign that form
for me, baby?'

And instantly he sits up and says, 'No. And get out of my bed.
That's *my* blanket you're stealing.'

So I stand up and I think it through. I have a choice here. On
the one hand, this awkward gawky free-market-fundamentalist
was the best lay of my life. It's a thin line between love and
hate, baby. But this is a matter of principle.

So I get dressed and go straight to Security. And Josh is kicked
offa campus before sundown. Expelled. And that night…guess
who's having dinner by herself.

So it's *hard,* okay? Like I said, we all make sacrifices. But later
that night…maybe I'm depressed, I don't know. But I go back
to the dining hall, just to clear my mind, be alone. And the
dining hall is totally deserted. And I'm just staring up at the
banner we got hanging there – it's the first thing you see – just

the slogan for our experiment, in big red letters, says: *WE FIND THE PROMISE IN PROMISCUITY.*

And I'm thinking, fucking Josh Rosenberg, I *hate* him but I'm thinking about what he said: *Freedom of Association.* We got this law, and it *looks* like the Experiment is working, but…nobody's using it for real progressive purposes. Are they?

God-damn Josh Rosenberg. He's not just *far* right. He might also be…right.

And I'm not just far-left, I'm getting…left behind.

And then I start to think about Eddie, and that club he took me to, Buzz or Fierce or whatever, felt great but I wasn't gonna get laid there, was I? It was liberating for *him*, but for me it was just – Britney Spears, *Slave 4 U.*

And now I'm standing alone in the dining hall at midnight, I just exiled Josh Rosenberg, I'm supposed to be filing forms, and – I'm not gonna get laid here, either.

'Cause if Josh is right: then Free Love is different from Free Association, and that's prejudice too. You gotta learn to…think outside the box.

Then I think, so where's Eddie right now? 'Cause it hits me: this is a typical liberal arts college, we got the typical gaggle of faggots – but they all slept with each other already and compared notes before we even *passed* the motion. They didn't need any legislation to be sluts. But I don't see any of *their* names on the paperwork, not Eddie, not any of his pipsqueak clique. Why aren't they experimenting? I mean, what are they doing tonight? *Facials*?

Well, if some people gotta think outside the box, all those gay boys, maybe they gotta start thinking – *inside* the box.

So I'm filling out a form, and filing it now. Tomorrow night. My bedroom. *Eddie.*

5. BRAD

Whoa.

Look, I know maybe you saw this coming but I didn't see it coming. I mean, when they described the policy I just thought, like, awesome. Like I got the Publishers Clearinghouse Letter that promised me a lifetime supply of free poonanny. So I sign up without reading the fuckin *fine print,* which is, uh –

Well, for starters, there's this – this gay thing.

Look, I'll be honest, it never even occurred to me that I was, like, a gay icon on campus? 'Cause, I mean, the, uh, the gay guys are not exactly in the same social set as me, y'know? Don't go to the same parties even. My world: Dave Matthews and beer. Theirs, uh, cosmos and Britney. (I *think.*) But I guess they've been watching me, through their binoculars – or, uh, opera-glasses – 'cause it's not long, man, it's not long before they figure out that I'm fair game.

And man, I am used to *pursuing.* I am used to pressing, bargaining, moving in for the kill, totally suave, one suave fuck, dude. I am used to being the fuckin *hunter-gatherer* here, clan of the cave pussy.

I am *not.* Used to bein *looked at.* As a, a – an object.

I am not used to bein looked at, period.

And another thing about being a hunter-gatherer is, is – the whole point of it is – you are unsuccessful ninety percent of the time. On average. I mean, the average guy. Me, I've got advantages, I'd say I'm unsuccessful more like seventy-five percent of the time, personally, but still –

Isn't that the *point?* I mean, I ran track and field in high school and I know there's nothing more – more frustrating than doing the hurdles and realizing when you come up to the next one that some *asshole* forgot to put out all the hurdles, and there's one missing, and so you have to *not jump*, that one time. I mean, if you think a hurdle is frustrating, you obviously have never encountered the *lack* of a hurdle, because that's really fuckin frustrating man.

This school is really fuckin frustrating.

This – this level-playing-field shit.

I mean, at first it was fun, askin all the girls I never got around to, a new one every night, and of course the girls who are askin me, the ones I never looked twice at, but that's kinda fun, too. I mean, nobody's gonna look down on you for who you sleep with, so why not, y'know, share the wealth, kinda. 'Cause I know what girls find hot. What girls find hot is when you fuck 'em and there's only one thing you can say afterwards, which is: *You're welcome.*

Before she even thanks you – 'cause you *know*.

You *know* how good you are.

Girls like a guy who's, well, cocky. And it's a matter of pride, making them feel like they're getting a superior experience because, well, because they are. And they know it. So I'm doin that, I'm lovin it…

Then it happens.

And by 'it', I mean – Eddie.

And I *totally* didn't see this coming, I get my schedule of who I gotta see, and it says that little Edward whatsisname, I mean, I barely even *know* this dude, he's making the request. And I gotta – just say yes. Like it's a *mandate*.

So I wait in my room. And I'm thinking – I don't know what I'm thinking. I mean, I took a shower and all, because that's what I always do, and I'm – okay, I'm thinking, maybe this is the time to make a run for it, get the fuck outta Dodge…But I guess I talk myself into staying because, well. This is new. I mean, I don't want you to think I've gotten *bored* of girls but

– well, I can say yes once. I mean, everybody else is saying yes to everything and nobody looks any the worse for it. Yet. And maybe it'll make me seem sensitive, tryin it. *Once.* So I just slap on some Polo cologne behind my ears till I smell like an eighth grade dance, and I sit on the edge of my bed, and I wait. And I don't even know what to do, I like – (*BRAD makes the sign of the cross, and clasps his hands.*) – no, seriously dude, I pray. Mean, I don't *actually* pray, but I try to remember the words: like fuckit, fuckit, *in the name of the father the son the holy* – *fuck* – how does it start? remember how it starts and –

Hail Mary.

The door swings open. Eddie.

So he comes in, and he says hi, and it's just – awkward. A lot of these dates have been awkward at first, I mean, especially with the geeky girls, like that Death Studies major, *boy* was that awkward, don't even *ask.* But Eddie sits down next to me on the bed and I – I can't even look at him. And the clock's ticking. And then he says – 'You wanna do this, or what?'

And I just say, 'You're askin me, dude, I gotta do it.'

I say it like I'm ready to bite the bullet. Or the pillow.

And he says, "Kay. You wanna kiss me?'

And when he says that I'm kinda relieved 'cause – well, that's not what I was expecting, and I guess I never even *thought* about it, I mean honestly it is so totally totally alien to my experience, so I guess it never occurred to me that, well, that homos like to kiss each other.

So, uh, I kiss him.

And it's just like kissing anybody else.

He's a tiny bit scratchy on the chin, just there, but his cheeks are soft, and – and in fact, I will admit this – not that I was turned on by it or anything – but I'll admit: he was a better kisser than most of the girls I've been with. He kissed – well, it was a little girly but underneath it was aggressive right back at ya. He kissed the way a guy imagines that a girl *should* kiss but that girls never do. Or, what you learn, is that the girls who *do* kiss that way are psycho. Boil your bunny after a *week.*

Then he breaks the kiss and he holds my face and he looks me in the eye.

And oh jeez, that scared me.

I mean I wanted to do anything *but* look him in the eye. And now he's not saying anything and I'm – fuckit, I'm *nervous,* man – so I just say what's on my mind.

I say: 'I guess you wanna fuck me up the, uh, butt, now, right.'

And he says, real fast, 'GOD no.'

And I'm relieved. Of course. But also a little offended, actually, 'cause I'm thinking, what, I'm not good enough for this wuss? What gives?

But he's lookin me right in the eye and he says, all breathy: 'I think *you*...should *definitely*...fuck *me.*'

And I mean, God, I know that's what – uh, people of Eddie's persuasion do to each other but it also never occurred to me that sometimes they *ask* to have it done. I guess I figured like, they flip a coin each time.

Then he leans down and unzips my fly and gets my cock in his mouth *immediately* and, well, I guess I was a little hard already, not from thinking about him, but because kissing is kissing, and skin is skin, and feeling somebody else warm next to you...you don't even think about whether they're your...your *type* in any way. You just get a chub-on.

I mean, that's the scary thing, isn't it? That potentially anybody's your type. Like, when your eyes are closed? There's no such thing as an insincere boner.

So he sucks me till I'm rock-hard, and then he stands up and wriggles out of his clothes, and I turn away and pull off my Eddie Bauer rugby shirt and slip outta my Levis and I turn back and he's already in this position, like, doggie-yoga-style: ass in the air, head against the mattress, and he's totally smooth, and really slim, and without looking too closely he practically looks like a girl, and I look down and see his – uh, his *hole* is just winking at me, and I think: Whoa. Normally I gotta *arm-wrestle* with the girl till I get to this point and here it is. I could get into this. Potentially.

So I slip on the condom and I spit in my hand and rub it on the end of my dick, and I put it right up against him and grab his hips, which are like a girl's, they're bony like a hot girl's hips, and I start to push in and then something like, *slooshes* up against me and I realize –

I realize it's his balls slapping against me, and I step back and I swear to god I start to gag.

And he knows something's wrong 'cause he swivels round and he's like, 'Are you okay?' And he's got this look in his eyes, and –

And I realize that I, uh, I offended him.

And I say, 'I'm sorry, I just – I – I'm *straight,* man.'

And he says, in this weird dreamy way, '*I know.*' Just like that. '*I know.*'

Like if I really am straight, that would make me…more attractive?

Which I totally don't get.

Then he says, 'Is there any way you – ?'

And honestly, I don't want to offend him. Like: what if that was me? Which of course it would never be me, not in a gazillion years, but that's not the important part: the important part's the *what-if.*

So I say, 'Yeah, sorry, man, just gimme a mo. I just thought – sorry – thought for a second I was gonna lose my lunch.'

And he says, 'Omigod, don't worry about it, I totally know what you mean. You should've seen *me* last night. When Lynette made me chow her box? *Oh-My-God*. But don't worry, you get over it.'

I don't say a word. But at that moment, I think: you fucking *bitch*.

Not him. Lynette. It's all her fucking fault. And that's when I feel it.

So I say to him, bend over and I go up, stick it in, and I fuckin *bang* his scrawny ass, and all I'm thinking's *back-and-THRUST, Lynette-you-BITCH, Lynette-you-BITCH*, till I finally cum.

And I pull out. And it's quiet. Mean, Eddie's quiet. I'm worried he'll never walk again. I have no idea what he's even thinking but he gets up, gets dressed, and – he turns and looks me. I'm sitting there. Still naked. Not saying anything.

And he whispers: '*Omigod*, thank you *so much*, that was *totally amazing*.'

Which, again, I totally don't get.

But I'm not even thinking about him, 'cause I'm, like, *possessed*. Mean, normally after I fuck, I like to chill, smoke a bowl, play some Xbox – but not tonight. Not now. This – thing comes over me. And I go to my desk where I gotta stack of the request forms and I write one out, *Lynette*, then I march to S-Cubed to file the fuckin form and inside me's – rage. As I walk through the cold, my breath's coming out like steam. I'm keeping it simmering. Hot. Like a fuckin *teapot*. Like a steam engine charging ahead. I go inside, and – Would you believe? She's the one at the desk. The only one there. And she hops up, starts saying something –

But I just slap down that form and march past her, peeling off my shirt, my boxers, like *I'm* a boxer, entering the ring, I roll on a condom like it's a boxing glove, and say: *Get naked.*

Then I go to her desk and just shove all the paperwork off. Like a fuckin New England blizzard. Then I turn around – And I throw her across the desk. I let her have it. I fuck her *so hard.* I fuck her like she's in my way and I'm tryin to *break through.* I nail, I pound, I fuckin *slam into her* and I shoot and pull out, stand up, look down at her on the desk, to see if she got the message.

And she smiles up at me and says, 'Wow. You must really be learning something. I *enjoyed* that. And I wasn't expecting to.' Says, 'I thought you were a lousy lay last spring. But this time – felt like a *real connection.* Thanks. You opened my mind.'

And I don't say anything. I get dressed, walk out onto the Quad, and it's cold, and it's snowing, first snow of the year. And I look up into the sky and shout it out –

I shout: Jesus Christ, if you can't fuck somebody for *revenge* anymore, then what's the fucking point of *anything?*

End of Act One.

Act Two

6. HELEN

Isn't this lovely? We all get a little break, then we come back for the start of the Spring Term. The second semester, the second chance. To change our opinions, expand our knowledge, and learn something new – to correct, repeat, revise.

But my favorite moment is now: as it's just beginning. January in Vermont, I'll stand at the window, in the lingering somber light, the bitter chill. And I look out onto the winter landscape of New England: the frost and the Robert Frost, the heavy snowdrifts, the heavenly whiteness – like the cool marmoreal chastity of the Parthenon. And – what am I forgetting?

Oh yes. Normally I wrap my shoulders in a woolly afghan, take my books and papers to huddle by the radiator to keep warm. But not tonight. Even in January, even in Vermont, even in this drafty old farmhouse, I don't feel the cold. Oh no...

'Cause I? Am the last of the Red Hot Bluestockings! Tssss!

Like a burlesque comedienne, HELEN licks a fingertip and touches it to her derrière, and makes a sizzling noise. Perhaps, keeping with the burlesque, she even drops her woolly afghan or winter clothing to reveal much more youthful attire beneath – nothing embarrassing. She should seem genuinely rejuvenated.

Ohhh, mercy me and goody goody gumdrops... What a joy, what a thrill, to discover at my age – not only does the plumbing still work, so does the *electricity!* It's been like a Spring Term for my life. Very educational, and – dare I say it? – *sexy.*

Perhaps that seems...unexpected? I hope not. I know that a university classics department is often chock-full of fulminating fuddy-duddies like Allan Bloom or Donald Kagan or Mary Lefkowitz or, or – whatsisname, a sound philologist but otherwise a complete madman – Friedrich Nietzsche.

Well, darlings, I'm not one of *them*. Have you even seen my syllabi? Horace's Eighth Epode. Juvenal Six. The infamous Honors Seminar on Aristophanes? If anyone could actually *read* this stuff, they'd call me a dirty old woman! I suppose that's why I decided to give it a whirl. Although my little gesture on the first day of class? Not an auspicious start, really. Only one student, Edward, Eddie, ended up taking the seminar. And among the students, Humanities 360-A is known as 'Going Down ON Ancient History.'

But never mind that. I'm a *student* now, committed to a new course of study. And a little learning *is* dangerous, so – I took the plunge. Diving in to the fountain of knowledge, only to learn – it's also the fountain of youth! And oh, my mind is *alive*...I keep thinking ...thinking: if only they'd known what I know, back then! The Trojan War would be settled with Greek Love. Helen of Troy would not have been marked with shame – she could just give head to save face! And that wise old virgin, Pallas Athena, would never have started the war, if she'd dropped that Apple of Discord, and...popped her cherry instead. It is *Utopia*!

Now I know what you're thinking. Has the professor lost her mind?

Oh no. No no no.

I did lose *something*, but it wasn't my mind...

Oh, but darlings, let me tell the story!

Now I admit I was nervous at first. But it turned out to be lovely. Brad was a perfect gentleman.

Before our – date, I had no idea what to expect. I warned
him in advance, it would be my first time. I didn't want to be
embarrassed in case he…had to brush away any cobwebs.

But when I opened the door and saw him, I knew – Brad was
taking this seriously. Like a good student, he turned up well-
prepared, with an open mind. And I could tell that he believed
a girl's first time should be special. Romantic. With a starched
blue button-down oxford-cloth shirt, tassel-loafers, *aftershave,*
darlings! and his hair pomaded back like Rudy Vallee. And he
brought some microwave popcorn, and…a videotape. *Titanic.*
The perfect date-movie, he says. 'Did you see it?'

I'm worried he means: did I see the *actual* Titanic go down
in 1912. Either way the answer is no, so Brad says: 'Great.'
And we switch off the lights, and sit there on the loveseat, and
watch those flickering images on the screen, like the cave-
dwellers in Plato's *Republic.* And the film begins, and we watch –

Some little old white-haired lady. Doddering about on
the deck of a salvage-vessel, prattling on about this vulgar
necklace, a jewel of great price she'd lost some eighty years
prior. I felt *so* self-conscious, and then – to make matters worse
– Brad stretches and yawns loudly. And I think: *oh no, it's
just as I feared – I'm old and plain and dull as a nun's slipper, and
Brad? He's just…not that into me* –

Until he finished his loud yawn-and-stretch and I felt his arm
fall around my shoulder! (Did you know boys still pulled that
stunt?) Then we snuggled close, and we watched the film, and
when the boat went down…so did I.

Then he whisked me off to the bedroom, and – it happened.
And happened. And happened. My word, these young men
have *stamina,* and – and oh, go on. Laugh if you want, I almost
wanted to laugh. Or cry. Because it *was* my first time. And
although Brad did his best – well. There's nothing sexy about
ignorance.

You don't know what to expect, so you rely on hearsay or
– or prejudice. Some girls expect pain and heartbreak, some
(I suppose) are terrified of pregnancy. And some think it
will offer transcendence, Olympian heights, Corybantic
ecstasy – then, all you get is a lot of awkward slippery thumb-
fumbling, I mean, at one point I thought I should offer to fetch
a flashlight.

When we'd finished, Brad kissed me on the top of the head,
told me he had a nine a.m. seminar, gotta run, see ya round,
got my digits? He dressed and tiptoed down the stairs…I got
up and walked to the window, wrapped in one of mother's
quilts. And I watched him go down the path, and back to
campus…

Then I spun around and dropped the crazy quilt, and I stood
in front of the mirror, stark staring naked, and threw out my
arms and whooped – *consummatum est!*

Really! It was the most fun I had in years. Because I was
learning about something new. And my lesson went well, all
things considered. True, it was embarrassing, or bewildering,
at times…but you don't begin piano lessons by tossing off
Rachmaninoff. You start by slowly fingering Anna Magdalena
Bach.

Because education begins with ignorance. The tabula rasa,
the uninscribed white snowdrifts of Vermont…virginal. Until
suddenly it's the Spring Term. When all the vivid colors start
poking up through the snowy blankness, the daffodil, the
crocus, until – there you have it, once again. Not Allan Bloom,
but – Spring in Bloom. A late-flowering spring – and late *de*
flowering, too – but I don't feel like an old lady, no, not in
the least. I feel like – Britney Spears. Because I'm one of the
students again, heart and soul. Although –

Although there's still the *mind*. Which can never be satisfied,
only exhausted… *lassata, necdum satiata.*

So. My restless mind still has one reservation, to wit…our goal is to *eradicate prejudice*. But is that possible? I think you can do as I have: correct your mistakes, learn new tricks, expand your knowledge.

But prejudice isn't knowledge, it isn't a *thought*, it's more like – an instinct. It's the thought you have *before* thought itself begins. So how can you hope to fight it? How can the liberty to bed somebody on a whim make any difference? When prejudice runs so deep, it calls the tune even for your whims. Does opening your mind, your heart, your legs – does that change what you are? We can revise our opinions, my dears, but not objective facts.

Look at me.

Look at me on my learning curve, or my slippery slope, and what do you think? *Instinctively.* Do you laugh? Do you want to laugh?

But you'd never dare laugh to learn a black girl has a crush on a white boy, would you? Even a gay boy in love with a straight – that's poignant, not laughable. And yet the laugh rises automatic in your throat when you hear a *spinster* has joined the dole-queue for her lawful allotment of pleasure, doesn't it? It's like the bitter jeering of Aristophanes, as he laughs at the vanity of human wishes, and mocks our Utopian hopes. See, the kids are putting the *promise* back in *promiscuity*. But this old crone is proving that only a *teen* can be a *libertine*. Even if she has squeezed a little *sex* outta *sexagenarian*.

Well, here I am. Look at me. Then laugh if you like. Laugh because I'm old. Then glance at your watches: you're getting older by the minute, darlings. The joke's on you.

Go on, take a closer look, you'll see: this woman hasn't lost her mind or reason. Just her cherry, and – what else? what more?

Her dignity?

Well, if that's what you're thinking – then shame on you. Where else can education begin? It starts with the awkwardness, the embarrassment, of adolescence. Even at my age, embarassment is the price of learning. You should embrace it as I have.

But my colleagues on the faculty here, self-important arrogant asses, think they have nothing to learn...so they're *mortified*. Skulking, shamefaced, hiding in shadows.

Well, they're not *all* embarrassed. There's Bob. (There's *always* Bob.) And maybe you know this type? Bob Gergen, and his wife Mindy. They're the openminded duo, models of academic freethinking. A married couple with – an 'open relationship.' Only on a college campus do you find such a pair, we've wondered about them for years. Bob and Mindy and...their 'marriage.' What is it? A tax shelter? It seems to provide very little shelter for their sullen thirteen-year-old daughter, who clearly detests them. And when you see all three Gergens, you cannot help but think – if you leave a marriage open long enough, surely something falls out?

So. That's Bob Gergen. Who stopped me on the steps of the library the other day. Marching across the quad, he hails me with one of his thick little arms, made muscular (no doubt) by years of swinging.

'Hey Helen,' he shouts. 'Face that launched a thousand ships!'

Let's be honest. I think Bob's a creep, and worse than that, I *know* he's a sociologist. But I wheel my bicycle over, and I say: 'Professor Gergen. Good morning.'

'I heard about what you did,' he says, grinning. 'Right on.'

'What I...*did*?' I say, rather glacially.

As befits a relentless lothario, Bob is incapable of embarrassment. It's *lethal.*

'What you did with your students,' says Bob. 'Same as the Ancient Greeks, I guess.' And he stares at me with those *hologram eyes*, the sort you find only among sex-addicts and born-again Christians, wanting to share the good news, share the *love*, with everyone they meet.

I stare back and say: 'Heavens, I hope you're not implying that you and I have the same paedagogical approach, Professor Gergen. There's a big difference between Plato's Republic and Plato's Retreat.'

He laughs and says, 'Seriously, Helen. When I heard about you doing tequila body-shots at the Winter Formal? Fishnets and miniskirt? That was... *unexpected.*'

I just smile and say 'Then Professor Gergen, that is *prejudice*. Age-ism, I think it's called?'

And he just says: 'Hey, it wasn't prejudice! It just got me thinking...if that was your Winter Formal, Helen, gimme a call when it's time for the *Spring Fling.*'

I just look at him and say: 'Don't be macabre.'

Then I mounted my bicycle and rode back to my house.

Was that rude of me? I've admitted I don't like him, but...like I said, no wisdom in ignorance. And here are the facts: once upon a time, Bob and Mindy Gergen had an open marriage. An – arrangement. And over the years, they went on like any other married academics, competing ruthlessly with each other – not just in swinging, they're *both* sociologists, as well.

Until...

One day Fate, more ruthless and more accurate than any social scientist, stepped in. And at the age of fifty, Mindy Gergen underwent a double mastectomy. And Bob saw no reason to change his ways. Not when they had an agreement... an *understanding*. Not when they had an open marriage. Which was also…a mixed marriage. Isn't that what *every* marriage is? A man and a woman. A mixed marriage.

That's why I stayed single and carefree. Look at me! I don't even care if you laugh because I'm laughing too, I'm having fun, I'm having *sex*. I'm having more sex than any of you, that's for sure – I should be laughing at you! And Socrates was right, what wild ecstasy it is! I *am* like one possessed by a δαίμων, or demon – like a Bassarid calling for madder music, stronger wine – I'm like a wild-haired Bacchante, like a Maenad, like – like –

A virgin. (Hey!) Touched for the very first time –

See? I'm dancing to *their* tunes now, the modern maenads, the material girls. When I was their age, what was even *on* the hit parade? And as I say the words 'hit parade' you must think – Christ, what did *she* listen to? Rudy Vallee? How old did she say she was?

Well, I was young once, back when this little ditty was topping the charts. Sing along with me if you know it…

She sings:

Gaudeamus igitur
Juvenes dum sumus
Gaudeamus igitur
Juvenes dum sumus

For those who don't know Latin, a loose translation from a loose woman. *Gaudeamus*, let us *rejoice*. Let us dance and drink and fuck and – be very merry. Rejoice. *Juvenes dum sumus*. While we're still *young*. And then – what? I'm forgetting –

What am I forgetting? I joke about this but seriously, some days I feel that I *am* up to the Z in Alzheimer's. Especially when I'm climbing into bed with a new person every night, forgetting names, forgetting faces…and yes, now I remember. The song.

Post jucundam juventutem

After a pleasant youth. In youth is pleasure...

Post molestam senectutem

After a troublesome, grievous old age. *Molestam* – an unwanted assault.

Nos habebit humus,
Nos habebit humus.

Then the earth will have us. The dirt, the dust, the clay, the grave. But the song says rejoice, rejoice – because you're young. So dance, drink, fuck, laugh – enjoy yourselves. Enjoy each other.

Or else just – do as I do. Keep forgetting something.

7. LYNETTE

LYNETTE addresses the student assembly from notecards.

Fellow students, good evening. And also any faculty here that – Mr and Mrs Gergen, hello. Oh, and Professor West. Welcome.

I'm thrilled that the senate has asked me to lead an old-fashioned Vermont-style town hall meeting. For the start of the second semester, the second term, of our great democratic Experiment. And before I start, let me just say: Congratulations. Our first term was fantastic. Well done. Big props, people. Or, as someone close to me might say, if he could be here today: *Mazel.*

But listen up. We're still working towards an Ideal here. I'm talking about Equality. So we have to keep learning, arguing, trying new things – because the Experiment isn't finished. Remember, America started out as an experiment.

because, like America, the Experiment isn't finished. In fact, it's only beginning.

Okay.

LYNETTE picks up a manila folder, and opens it.

Now the Senate and the faculty adviser have asked me to make some remarks. And these are – questions, really. Submitted to the Complaints Bureau at SSS, and basically, I'm gonna take a look at these and offer my thoughts. And since Professor Gergen just handed me this file, I'll be doing this sorta off-the-cuff, but –

But basically, these are more serious than the usual questions we get, about whether you can make a vegan eat pussy. Or, is semen on the Atkins Diet? Should we put a stop to nocturnal emissions as a waste of valuable community resources? And if so, what happens to a wet dream deferred? Does it *explode*?

But these are questions about – enforcement. And look, I *hate* that word, but the fact is – we passed a law. And a law without enforcement's not a law. It's just nice words on a piece of paper. So. Here goes:

LYNETTE reads from a page in the folder.

'I'm having sex with a girl. She's a Philosophy major, I do Biology. She says to me, I'm getting bored, I don't *need* to have an orgasm. Ergo, you should stop.

And I say to her, I'm not trying to make you cum, I'm trying to make *me* cum. And she says: If I don't need to, then you don't need to either.

Then she gives me a lecture about post-feminist Hegelian teleology, which is boring so I just tuned out and kept humping till I came.

Did I do the right thing?'

Right. Um. Okay.

And look, I don't know who wrote this up at the top, but
this boy's got a serious question. So I don't need somebody
writing: 'Need-Blind Emissions Policy, Question Mark'

What this boy is talking about is – uh, some kind of biological
difference between men and women. I think. But from the
sound of it, you guys did the right thing. You gave it the
old college try. 'Cause you keep the argument going , that's
democracy in action.

Okay, now this... This one is interesting.

> 'I sent a request form, he arrived at my dorm room, we started
> making out but he couldn't get hard. When I told him to get an
> erection, he closed his eyes and started playing with himself. He
> was clearly thinking of another girl, who was probably thinner
> than me, with bigger boobs, but I don't know that for a fact
> because he wouldn't fess up when I started grilling him. So I told
> him not to imagine anybody but me, and he instantly lost his
> boner and we did not have sex. As a result of this, I felt *totally
> violated.*'

Right. You felt violated for a reason, girl. Because this – is the
new date rape. It's the new form of masculine aggression, and
it's called *impotence.* So if this boy is here tonight, lemme tell
him: Your penis is a selfish bigot. I don't have to see it to know
that it veers to the right. Shame on you.

But if this girl is here, listen up: you were wrong too. Why do
you care what he's thinking about. His imagination is off-
limits. You have his body, why do you want his mind? Because
you want total control, and that is not sexy or cool. So shame
on you, too. A vagina like that deserves to be called a Bush.

Look, this is supposed to be *fun,* okay? I don't know what to
say. I can't *legislate* a boner. Look, the snack bar in the student
center has got Viagra now. And girls, there's KY too, in a
variety of flavors. Fake it till you make it. Okay?

And also – maybe I should mention this – but I think we'll
have a way to solve all these problems very soon. Which

you'll find out in a very short while, later this semester. Right now it's a surprise but look. I know a lot of you have noticed that we took over the Theatre Building on campus, and we're renovating it. We even had some complaints about that, but I explained: just like the new rules made the Gay and Lesbian Student Alliance obsolete, so y'all got disbanded…well, for the same reason, we don't need a theatre anymore. Now that everybody can get laid at will, there is no rationale for undergraduate drama.

So, what we're doing with the theatre, we'll unveil after break. But I just wanna tell you, that when it's done, I think we'll have a solution for problems like this boy, and this girl, and all of you. The new theatre might help you all improve your performance.

Okay, and lemme see –

Who put this here?

Okay. Okay, fine, you want me to read this out loud? I'll read it out loud.

> 'I have a complaint. The rule is that I can't say no. But my idea of consensual sex is not *just* that both people say yes. It's that they could also say no if they wanted to. But now I am not allowed to say no to anyone. Therefore, I am not actually giving genuine consent to anyone. Therefore, everything that has taken place here is rape.'

Well. What am I supposed to say to that?

And I wasn't planning to name and shame, Mrs Gergen, but what am I supposed to say?

You signed the fuckin *form*, lady, that's why it's not rape. There's a difference between saying no, and – negativism. And that's what *this* is. You're killing our buzz. If you're not enjoying the party, then leave. Go. Get thee to a nunnery, I don't care. Because honestly –

Honestly, everybody knows what your situation is. Your husband'll fuck anything with a hole, I wouldn't trust that man with a bagel. But you're the one that *married* him. Why are you complaining to me? I've *empowered* you. You can fuck whoever you want.

And oh yeah. That's *great*. Get up and walk out. 'Cause you don't want to hear it. Fine. Just remember what I said: you can fuck whoever you want, Mrs Gergen. I suggest you start with yourself.

Guess that's meeting adjourned, people.

So yeah. The new theatre building, we're just waiting on the Fire Marshall to check it out. Then the fun is gonna start. Although please remember: fun is not the point.

8. BRAD

I'm gonna be honest about everything that happened. 'Cause they're still going on campus, back from Spring Break, but I – well, I dropped out.

And to start on being honest, lemme say honestly: I don't really like Lynette. It's a sign of respecting her, I can finally admit that.

I don't like her, but I have come round to her way of thinking. 'Cause she's the one who said it: fun is not the point.

And look, I knew I was missing the point. 'Cause it was all fun, all the time, and – I wasn't enjoying myself. So what *is* the point?

So I started doing it like – like it was community service. Charity work. Like, y'know, in the past I'd go sit in the library to scope out hot girls I hadn't scored with yet…but now I'd go there and try to find – the opposite. If it turns me off, I bust a move. And I'd saunter over, say…'Hey there, I'm Brad. You're

– *Cynthia?* Whatcha doin later, Cyn? Waxing your back? You wanna come over and do mine when you're done?'

But the surprising thing is that, well, even with that kinda girl, old habits die hard. I don't wanna fuck a nasty fat chick? Well, guess what, she's not all that comfy getting undressed with *me*. But then both of you do it, because you have to, and you manage to have a decent time. And seriously, have you ever had sex with somebody who was really, really fat? It's kind of – interesting. There's this, like, *bulk*, I mean, I always thought it would be like…like swimming, in a bad way. But really it's not. It's more like – I dunno – sculpting? I kinda got into it.

So then, I started to think about what could I *not* get into. What did I honestly *not* want. And that's what I'd do next. And this was the turning point…

I called Eddie. Sent a request for him.

Because there's something I do *not* want, something really hard to do. But also I'm thinking Eddie because – well, lemme say it. I'm thinking revenge.

So I request him and I shower, but – no Polo cologne this time. Fuck him. This isn't a *date*.

When he comes over, he's like 'Wow, I was kinda surprised, Brad.'

And I'm like, 'Why?'

And he's like, 'Well, 'cause you're *straight*.'

And I'm like, 'Straight is as straight does, dude. I fucked a girl this afternoon, then soon as I'm done, I ask for you.'

And he's like, 'So you're saying you're…experimenting? Or what, you're *bi*?'

And I say, 'I'm *nothing*, man. You know who I fucked this afternoon? *Cynthia Baca*.'

And his jaw just drops open, 'cause everyone knows her, mean, she's referred to informally as Chew Baca, 'cause she's, well, she's pretty much spherical and the face ain't much to look at either. And I say to Eddie, 'I asked for her, then I asked for you, so you tell me what I am.'

And he says, 'How could you want both me and – her?'

And I say: 'Cause it's not about what I want. I mean, does anybody even like Cynthia Baca?'

And he's like, 'She's one of my best friends, actually.'

And I say, 'Of course she is, how much more predictable could you get? That's why God *created* faggots, so the fat girls would have somebody to talk to at the prom. But tell me: if she's your friend, Eddie, why didn't *you* take one for the team and fuck her?'

And he's like, 'First off, do *not* say faggot, that offends me. And second, I wouldn't do that because – it's not...who I am.'

And I say, 'Yeah? You think it's who *I* am?' (Oh, he's pissing me off.)

And he says, 'Get real. Enough beer, straight guys'll stick their dick in *anything*.'

And I say: 'Now you're offending me. That is a *stereotype*.'

And he says: 'Oh, come on, you know that's true! It's not a stereotype – it's *identity*. It's... how we define ourselves.'

So I look him straight in the eye.

Then I pull off my shirt, drop it, unbutton my jeans, slip down outta them, so it's just my boxers and – me. And look him straight in the eye and say: '*Fuck me up the ass.*'

And he says, 'What?' Timid, like.

And I say: 'You heard me, tiger. It's all fuckin *fun and games* around here until somebody loses an identity. So I think *you*...should *definitely*...fuck *me*. I never tried it, but – *duh*. You know that. And it's not who I am. But what's funny is: it's not who *you* are either, Eddie – is it? So that's why I'm gonna *force* you. Now take off that frickin Belle & Sebastian tee-shirt and come over here and fuck me like a stud.'

And he's not – moving. Just staring.

So I slip off the boxers, and I lay on my back, butt-naked on the bed, and hold my legs up and open so he can stare at my hole and I say: 'Fuck that ass, Eddie. Do it like it's your *job*.'

And he looks like he's gonna cry and I say, 'Are you a man or not?'

And that does it. He steps forward, undoes his jeans, but – he's got, like, a *negative* erection. He's *terrified*. And there's only one way I can think of, to get him started. I suck his dick.

And it's not what you'd expect. It doesn't taste like anything. It's not sexy. It's like – like having some kinda big loose piece of macaroni in your mouth. Till he starts getting a boner, then it's like having somebody's thumb in your mouth, only bigger. It wasn't *hot*, though. I –

I don't know why girls do it, to be honest.

But when I say bigger than a thumb, I mean: Way Way Bigger. Mister Ed is hung like a horse, I mean, this kid has, like, a *gi-normous* cock. I'm talkin French Bread, Baby's Arm, Mel-Gibson Lethal Weapon.

So I'm wondering why doesn't he – wanna use it? I mean, if I had a piece like that, I'd be whipping it out all the time, but – maybe he doesn't want to hurt anybody? That's my guess. 'Cause he – he starts pushing in *gentle*, and, oh my fucking God, it is like slowly sitting down onto a orange traffic cone. Or, uh, giving birth. I dunno. It's like nothing I've ever even imagined, so I don't know. All I know is: somehow it's *worse* that he's being gentle.

And fuck it, I wanna show him what a man I am. How much I can take. If he's gonna use the Lethal Weapon, then I'll show him The Passion of the Christ.

So I shout IS THAT THE BEST YOU CAN DO? NAIL ME HARDER, FAGGOT!

And when I say that, he starts – *pounding*. And it fucking hurts, man. But so what. Everything hurts.

But God almighty this goes from like – like just plain hurting, like a toothache, into like – actual *Marathon Man* dentist-drilling agonizing *agony*, until –

Until he just – stops.

And I'm like, WHAT? YOU DON'T LIKE MY ASS?

And he says, 'I came.'

And that's – well, that's another thing I never knew. They can't feel it when you cum inside them. I always assumed they could, like it was like – purple fireworks going off inside your ass. But no. It's just – y'know, end of the ride, the movement stops. Game over, man.

And all I can think is, Welp, guess I should call up Jamie, let her know I *empathize*.

Then I look at Eddie and I see. Without saying anything, he just starts putting on his clothes but I notice, as he's getting dressed, he's – *crying*.

I just sit on my bed and wait for him to leave. Thinking – *whatever*. You're not a faggot anymore, faggot. And the way I see it: that's how I got my revenge.

Was I into it? No. Am I queer? No way. Then what was it?

Proof. That none of this is any fun. Proof that fun is not the point. 'Cause –

Look, did you ever see *The Matrix*?

Man, I *love* that movie. It's *so* intellectual. I totally wrote my college admissions essay about that movie, I was like, why do I want to go to college here? *Because I want to take the red pill, man.*

And it says something that I love that movie and it's deep. It's *philosophical.*

'Cause imagine if your brain was hooked up to a big computer. And I'm not talking virtual reality, I'm talking *real* reality. Like *The Matrix.* So what if the computer says: *your wish is my command.* Do you understand what I'm saying here? Anything you want – you get. You're hungry, you want a McFish Sandwich, and there it is – the Matrix gets you a McFish. And it's exactly what you wanted, hits the spot, yum. It's like a miracle. Instant gratification.

Okay, so if you're following me…imagine you could have anything *sexually.* The Matrix is gonna feed *that* appetite. So you think to yourself: okay, I wanna fuck…Insert Fantasy Here. Like I'd probably say that chick from *The OC?* But you can have anybody you want. Abe Lincoln. Anybody.

Think about it.

'Cause if you're a guy like me – it's biology, you think about sex every five minutes. But what would happen if you *got it* every five minutes? Whoever, whatever you want… it's like you're God.

Except – wouldn't you get bored?

'Cause you're not God. You're just – you. Like, compared to God, my interests are pretty limited. I got limitations. I'm boring. And even fun isn't fun. So after a while – maybe the only thing I would want is…not to want anything.

So after Eddie left, I just…lay there. Not wanting to move, not wanting anything. Then I think: I should get the hell off campus – if I can walk. I wanna get as far away as possible – and I walk down towards the town, just – humming, y'know,

Billy Joel song. About Catholic girls who won't have sex 'cause maybe they had the right idea.

'Cause I've done it all now, and it's like it didn't even touch me. Eddie fucked me so deep but he never got – *inside*? You know what I mean. Something's always there, untouched, hopeful...loving, even...and needing love...but so totally *absolute* about love that what could ever satisfy? Even if I slept with everybody in America, like the fuckin Sexual Miracle of Democracy, still – I won't get at the total mystery of what's inside. Inside me.

Like, my soul.

And I look up, and I realize I'm outside – an actual Catholic church? And thinkin bout my soul? And hummin the Billy Joel? Like, what the *fuck*, man. This is some kinda – *sign.*

So basically that's what happened. I dropped out of school, and – Dad really shit himself, 'cause of all the things he worried I might pick up in college nowadays – this? Fuckin' blindsided him. But it's not a totally done deal yet, 'cause –

'Cause the seminary is a little skeptical. About me, that is. But we're gonna make some kinda deal, right now we're armwrestling, bargaining, and they know: I'm not skeptical about one thing. I wanna be celibate.

And look, I know what's up, all the stuff in my past, I could be a big PR problem for the church, becoming a parish priest. But here's the deal: if it's not the seminary, then they told me – *Monastery*? Definitely an option. Sweet little monastery, top of a mountain, and all you do there is Ski, and Pray –

Monastery or else I could be – and this isn't a joke, this is seriously the term for it – a 'lay brother'.

'Cause I wanna be able to say that I formed lasting relationships at school. Isn't that why you go to college? Networking?

Well, I formed a lasting relationship with Our Lord. That's what I wanna say.

I wanna say: I'm nobody's bitch but God's.

9. HELEN

I said I loved the spring term. A chance to learn something new – and it's all new to me, a brave new world of…Britney Spears.

But a second semester, a second chance is not always better. It can be: *hit me baby one more time.* Or else it's: *oops I did it again.* I say this because – the police, the arrest, the impending trial. They have shut down the school while we wait to see what happens. That poor girl. I remember her name, but I can't remember…was she black? She's definitely in prison. Poor Lynette.

But I can't tell you much more about how it happened: as usual, I had my face buried in my studies. And – I was learning something.

Let me put it this way. In Plato's *Republic*, the story is told (by Cephalus) that Sophocles was asked near the end of his long long life – *What does it feel like to finally lose your sex drive?*

And Sophocles responded that he felt like a slave who has escaped, after many years of servitude with a mad and cruel master.

I understand that now. We talk about sexual liberation. But if the first lesson's all about letting loose, then I'm ready for the next lesson. The second semester. Where liberation means being freed *from* sex. Hallelujah, free at last.

So. I have come full circle. And I still proved I'm no square. But I know sex isn't my thing – I'm a little old lady who likes Greek verbs.

But I did come down from the Ivory Tower, for a bit. I wallowed. And now – I've passed through the madness and indignity of desire to emerge on the other side, bruised and weary but nonetheless – intact.

I'm post-sex. Or, as the young people would say, I'm so totally over sex.

Because what I learned. Sex isn't love. You knew that.

And these days I know it too because – I'm head over heels *in* love. Platonic love. But my dears, I need to tell you! Because I want you to know. And in case you thought I might end up old and alone. I didn't. I know I thought it – but I didn't end up old and alone. I'm – in a relationship. Going steady. We're *pinned!* To be honest, we're pretty much married. I know it sounds unexpected but…trust me. He's the one.

Since the college has been shut down and its future seems uncertain? I have taken, into my house here, Edward. Eddie. My lone student. Who is now, inexplicably, my sweet snugglepoozer as well.

It actually happened – right at the end of April, actually, it was right before the police turned up on the campus. That's why we missed all that drama, Eddie and I. We were at home, together.

I remember precisely. Twilight, one of those elongated evenings, I was in the house, making herbal-rosehips tea with spring water and honey, when the doorbell rings. And when I open the door, there he is. Looking so forlorn, like an immaculately-groomed urchin.

'Eddie!' I say. 'I know my memory's not what it once was, but…did we have a tutorial scheduled?'

He only says, quietly: 'Professor? May I come in?'

'Of course,' I said. 'Is something the matter?'

Then he looks up at me, with doleful eyes, and he says…
'I don't know who I am.'

Well now. I've heard that one before – my mother died of Alzheimer's, after all. So I know how to handle this sort of thing: you can't reason with that sort of panic, so, you needn't say a word. It's better simply to – reassure them, really. So I open my arms to hold him, and he fell into the embrace, resting that immaculately-tweezed brow on my bosom, as I stroked his precisely-gelled Caesar-cut. And we hold each other for a moment.

I just say, 'There, there.' And I'll know it's Alzheimer's if he says 'Where?'

But no. Eddie says, slowly and quietly: 'I don't know who I am, but… I *like* who I am when I'm talking to you.'

And I smiled and said, 'In that case, come into the kitchen with me. Let's talk.' And that's what we did, on into the night. And at last, we did what we have done every night since then.

Wordlessly, we clamber together into the vast laminated-rosewood faux-Renaissance Belter bed which I inherited on mother's death, the bed in which I was conceived (think of that!), and Eddie and I cling to each other. And here, in my drafty old Vermont farmhouse, we keep each other company, and we keep each other warm. That's all.

Oh, and occasionally we conjugate. Don't titter if you don't know what that means. In the dark we go through the forms of a Greek verb, laying out methodically and by rote the person, number, tense, voice of a dead language. Just for kicks.

Παιδεύω, I teach.

Παιδεύεις, you teach.

Παιδεύει, he, she, it teaches.

One night as we're doing that, I said to him: 'Snuggle, do you think this is strange? That we do this?'

And he said, 'Not at all – it's our conjugal bed.'

Isn't he grand?

And it *works*. That's the wonderful thing. Education, intimacy, love – without the sex. Eddie and I sleep together with what Petronius called 'socratica fides,' the Socratic trust, Socratic faith, the chaste love that Socrates felt for Alcibiades.

And I know it sounds a little crazy but – that's why it's love. Remember what Socrates himself said:

Τὰ μέγιστα τῶν ἀγαθῶν ἡμῖν γίγνεται διὰ μανίας

The greatest of blessings comes to us through…through *madness*. And these days I'm just – mad about the boy. Platonically. It's a marriage of the minds. No sex, no children, no shared checkbooks. We do get smoochy on occasion, but really it's just – a very civil union. Companionship. Conversation. Holding hands by the fire as the embers die down, until we're…ready to depart. And I won't be ready to do that for a while, dears. I'm only sixty-eight. But still –

I say to Eddie sometimes, I say: 'Snugglepoozer?' I poke him in his adorable pierced bellybutton and say 'Snugglepoozer? I have still got my health but the fact remains, I'm no spring chicken. So what if one day, I wind up totally gaga? If I retire from the faculty, and then my faculties retire from me, and I sail past the Z in Alzheimer's and end up like my mother?

And Eddie says: 'Just don't end up like *my* mother. And don't worry, Helen. I'll love you no matter what.'

And I say: 'But what if we can't have these conversations? If I've forgotten all my Greek, if we can't foozle in bed and – conjugate? Eddie. It's a serious question. What if the Alzheimer's hits me on my next birthday? Will you still need me, will you still feed me, when I'm sixty-nine?

And he says: 'Helen, even if that happened, which it won't, even if you don't remember who I am, who you are, don't remember anything at all... I'll still love you. But I have to ask him – why? And Eddie says – You need a reason? I'm sure I can find something to love you for, even when your mind is gone...'

'Like what?' I ask. 'I'm assuming it's not my figure.'

And Eddie says: 'Honey! Don't you know? Boys like me just *love* to go antiquing.'

So sweet!

And he says: 'How's this? I'd love you for being the *ultimate* absent-minded professor.'

'Edward,' I say, 'That is a *stereotype*. Prejudice!'

Then he giggles and says: 'Okay. Think of it this way. Once your mind is gone? I can also say, Look! Someone has finally done it! This wonderful woman has totally eradicated prejudice. In fact, she's so open-minded her brain fell out!'

And then we laughed and foozled and – I'm not wrong about him, he's a keeper. He's clever, right? He's funny. When he's with me. When we're together, we are – everything to each other.

But that's what true love is, don't you think? Where you can't even tell. Which one's the teacher, which the student, which one the parent, which the child – I mean, honestly, who cares? We're simply...rejoicing, Eddie and I. We rejoice.

10. LYNETTE

Like a lotta folks, the biggest mistake I ever made was getting involved with undergraduate drama. 'Cause it all started with the theatre.

We took the drama building, to use it for – something else. Something more radical. Well, more radical than the Spring

Musical, which we cancelled. And we rebuilt the student theatre as one big dark room...but comfortable. There's pillows, swings, divans and benches, you'd just relax and sink in. Total darkness. Just a whole lotta people finding themselves together in a state of pure perfect divine ignorance, and you take the plunge, dive into these depths – losing yourself, finding yourself – in...this room. A genuinely Egalitarian Educational Experiment. Although the students just called it the Orgy Room. Then somebody makes the joke, they start calling our theatre 'Lynette's Big Black Box'. Which is actually pretty funny. So I wasn't offended.

And the Fire Marshall checked it out, we had lesbian stagehands to put those little glow-strips round sharp corners, and along the perimeter. We bought glow-in-the-dark condoms, even.

And the idea was simply that you'd go into the theatre, the Orgy Room, and you'd never know who was there, or what might happen, besides love. Love with – with someone. Black or white, straight or gay, boy or girl, you'd just start – *loving*. Making love, in whatever position you wanted, from Missionary down to John Rawls Original, Doggy-Style or Daisy-Chain, Tantric or Texas Pile-Driver, it wouldn't make any difference, because –

Because you couldn't see a thing in there. Love is blind, right?

But more than that, I wanted to think of our new space like a *laboratory*. For our experiment with an idea of pure democracy. Because love is blind but this was double-blind, like research. Who knows? In the dark like that, maybe we will accidentally invent a new sexual position.

Actually, that's what I was hoping for. 'Cause the truth is, we were all getting kinda bored with sex. Even me.

I don't know why. Maybe total freedom is boring. Maybe – maybe there's a reason why college students grow up. I don't know. I just kept hitting my head against the same damn problems.

Like this one girl, sorta Goth, who always said she was majoring in Death Studies, she came to me, in tears. All that black eyeliner smeared across her face, and she says to me, 'I just can't keep *doing* this. I'm ugly. Nobody would say yes to me without these rules. But after I graduate...I'll still be ugly. So what happens then?'

And I *wanted* to say, You know, yeah, you *are* kinda ugly, it's the overbite, but somewhere out there? Somebody's gonna think you're attractive. It's not like being *black*. Ugly is subjective.

But I hafta be sympathetic, so I say, 'Well hey, girl. I find you attractive.'

And she stops crying and looks at me *nasty*, and says, 'Spare me the Alice Walker horseshit. That's worse. 'Cause I don't find *you* attractive at all.'

What the fuck?

Or even Eddie starts having some kinda existential crisis, says: 'Lynette, I thought I knew who I was – I had an identity. I knew that when I left school, I would be marginalized – marginalized and *fabulous*. But now, who am I?'

And I wanted to say, Marginalized? Who you fooling? A gayboy at a four-year liberal arts college in Vermont – you're practically *mainstream*.

But I'm *nice*. So I say, 'Well, I'm a black woman, baby. Don't you think maybe I'm in the same position?'

And he looks at me, *really* bitchy, and he says: 'Well, you didn't exactly have to tell your mother you were black, Lynette.'

And I start thinking, what the hell is this? Some kinda victimization sweepstakes? What happened to feeling like

– like we could be *anything?* Isn't that what we came to college *for?*

But you have to have a self before you can *be* yourself, I guess. So nobody really wants that freedom.

So I'm thinking, we need something radical here. A kick in the ass. So I go to the senate, and I say: Look. Let's forget the Spring Fling, let's do something revolutionary, let's get everybody in the Orgy Room at the same time. On the First of May, Mayday, we'll celebrate the rites of spring, *plus* the radical equality that unites the human race!

So we make the plans. And everyone's there, pretty much. I know because I'm the one checking names as they go in, making sure they leave their clothes and their prejudices at the door. So it's just all those nice people in the dark – you just go in, give in, go down, give head, go crazy, naked, relaxed, aroused, touching, tasting, together in a big black box where everyone's *equal.*

After I got all the names, I take off my clothes and join them.

As naked and ignorant as the day you were born, so full of *possibility.* It's like Stevie Wonder in a room fulla groupies.

So I walk in and – right away there's a tap on my shoulder from behind, I turn around, and suddenly – I'm kissing somebody. I don't do a crotch-grab, or even a boob-check. Just – hands against hands, and lips against lips, thinking: this kiss is shy and aggressive at the same time, it's like – like kissing *myself,* the first time I ever kissed someone, back in junior high. We could be anything, you and I. Then –

Bang, the door flies open, the light snaps on, and the whole room turns to look.

There. In the doorway. Mrs Gergen.

She's walking straight into the room, unstoppable, past the Goth Chick who's in a daisychain with the Senate Secretary and a dyke stagehand…past Becky Haslanger with half of the lacrosse team – they found her in the dark? And Mindy Gergen walks past my freshman roommate Jamie, who's doing the lesbian scissors with Cynthia Baca, who's blowing Bob Gergen, who is wincing at Cynthia's toothy technique. He looks up at his wife. She doesn't look at him.

Because she's walking toward me.

But she's not looking into my eyes. It's like she's looking at something else.

And she is. The person I've been kissing. Her thirteen-year-old daughter. Who starts laughing like any rebellious thirteen-year-old that's found the best way to piss off her mom.

Mrs Gergen grabs the girl, runs out of the theater, and –

Everybody looks at me. I don't even know what happened next. I remember standing there. Alone. In the middle of the theatre. As the sirens come howling. As the cops drag me out. And the cameras, photographers, local news are there to see me in handcuffs. And I'm naked, so the cops cover me up. With some American flag.

I'm sure you've all seen the photo – it's a great story for the local news. I'm not the *stereotypical* black person under arrest. Oh no. I'm something special: Miss All-American Pervert Intellectual, the corruptor of youth. Honest, I'm just waiting for the warden to hand me an ice-cold fo'ty full of *hemlock*.

And in my cell I'm thinking: love is blind, equality's blind, but guess what? Justice is supposedly blind too…but there are some prejudices you can never get past. 'Cause it's a visceral reaction. Like instinct. Just think about – maternal instinct. That's what Mindy Gergen had. And that's why everybody gets so worked up about higher education. You give your child to some strange new mother with crazy ideas: an *alma mater*.

But frankly, that kind of prejudice – the gut instinct kind, like – like maternal instinct? Even if that *is* prejudice, it's also what saved my ass.

Because there I am, alone, locked up in solitary, no-one will speak to me, until –

Until I make that one phone call.

My mom flies up to Vermont. B A from Barnard, J D from Harvard, she's a *lawyer*, remember? And she's a pro bono deus ex machina, straight outta Greenwich.

So she sits down with me in the visiting room at the prison, and says: 'Lynette? You wanna tell me what you were doing?'

And I said: 'I'm like Socrates, Mom. I'm an intellectual with radical ideas, they get scared, accuse me of kiddy-fiddling and lock me up.'

Mom says: 'Socrates was an intellectual 'cause he was *totally ignorant.* So I can see the resemblance.'

Damn, she's good.

But I decide to be honest, I say: 'Mom, I just wanted to feel…*possibility.* Like I could be anybody, *anything.* Like it doesn't matter if I'm male or female, straight or gay, black or white…then I get arrested for molesting some kid.'

And Mom looks at me and says: 'Who are you? Are you my daughter, or are you – *Michael Jackson?*'

And I said, 'I'm your daughter. Are they gonna convict me?'

And Mom says, 'I'm your lawyer, and I'm your mother, so lemme tell ya, Michael. Together, we're gonna *beat it.*'

Well, as you can imagine, Mom's a *very* good trial lawyer. She's a mother, a moral authority, and middle class – she's warm, sympathetic, smart enough, and she's not afraid to cry – omigod she *is* Oprah Winfrey. Just like Oprah, sex is the last thing on Mom's mind. This case is not about sex, says mama. It's all about – *education*. Where does a little girl learn to sneak into places she shouldn't? From her parents, those liberal academic types, with their alternative lifestyle? If you don't blame these liberal parents, says Mom, who else you gonna blame? Britney Spears?

My God! She's blaming the victim! What's next?

It's like Mom's modern middle-class minstrel show! She does everything but fuckin *moonwalk* to show that jury that her baby's smooth, but no criminal. But all that pales next to her grand finale. She gets up for her closing, and –

Mom plays the Race card. 'Cause look at her. She knows *nothing* trumps the Queen of Spades.

First she's silent. Until you realize she's got real tears streaming down her cheeks. Then she speaks: 'Ladies and gentlemen, that is my baby up there. And she's got no idea how much I *love* her. Because I – *am her mama*. I know she's totally ignorant. But that don't mean you gotta teach her a lesson: I'm her mama, let me do that. But please oh please, don't give my baby a life sentence. Only a mama can give her baby life. Don't you give her life.

And I'm just thinking, goddamn, I *know* this jury's gonna give me life now, just 'cause my mama gave them *Imitation of Life*.

But there's not much evidence, so the jury reaches a verdict pretty quick: *Not Guilty*. It's not the first time I got off in Vermont, but here's hoping it'll be the last.

As we're driving home, I said, 'Mom, what the *fuck* was that?'

And my Mom says: 'That was me saving your ass. So grow up, Lynette. It's the way things are. Doesn't matter if you're a Harvard lawyer from an expensive suburb. When white folks see you, they think, *hey, I bet she sure can sing and dance*. So I gave them a song and a dance.'

I say, 'You did everything but get down on your knees like Jolson.'

Mom says, 'Worked, didn't it? Besides, I did it to teach you something. The only thing that stands between you and your ideals is people's *ignorance*. And there's only one way to deal with ignorance.'

I'm glaring at her, and say: 'What's that?'

Mom says: '*Become a teacher.* Just like your precious Angela Davis. Start out a student radical, end up a tenured professor. It's not a bad lifestyle, honey – benefits, healthcare, three months off every year, sabbaticals – '

So. I learned my lesson. It's good to have a mother. And you're nice people, you all had mothers too. I assume. And I'm glad that my mom had sex *once*, though you wouldn't think it to see her. That one time is the reason I'm here.

'Cause it does only take one time. 'Cause…uh…by the way? I'm pregnant. When I found out, first thing I think is: I'm gonna *love* fuckin with those stereotypes… *Yeah, I'm nineteen years old. Yeah, I'm a African-American unwed single mother. No suh, I don't know who my baby's daddy is, wasn't really payin attention, could be a lotta folks. And what's that? Do I have an arrest record? Yes'm. I was arrested once. For rape, but I got off.*

Then they meet me, and – I blow their minds.

That would be funny, but – actually I *do* know who the daddy is. It's Josh Rosenberg. So I called him and he took the train up to Greenwich, we went out for coffee, and *of course* we started to argue immediately, but then we suddenly realized – this would be a perfect marriage. It's sexy. It would never be predictable. And both of us could really, *really* piss off our parents.

And look, I know this sounds crazy. Crazier than anything else I did at college. But what can I say? Opposites attract. He's libertarian, I'm egalitarian – he's from Mars, I'm from Venus – he's Jewish, I'm black. But he's willing to convert.

So we're getting hitched – just a civil thing down at City Hall, but you should come find us afterward, come to our party. And wish us luck, people, 'cause we'll have the baby, and finishing up our college degrees at the same time. We decided to transfer – to Brandeis. That's where Angela Davis went. Did you know that? I didn't till Josh told me. Funny, she doesn't *look* Jewish.

So that's it. I guess it sounds crazy. But I'm looking forward to marrying Josh. 'Cause I love to fight, and you *know* we're gonna fight. We'll argue. Isn't that the point? That's what marriage is. That's what democracy is too. You only know you're married because you disagree, you get angry, you care enough to argue. But you know in your hearts that this is – a partnership, between equals. And you know you love each other.

Still, even me and Josh can find some things to agree about like – equality, and freedom, and love, and – loving our *baby*.

Even if that baby is male or female, black or white, straight or gay – who knows? Who cares? We won't.

'Cause we'll be parents then. Which means that me and Josh, right or wrong – right or left even – are gonna look into those eyes and say: *Baby, the possibilities are limitless…you can be anything in this world… Anything.*

And: *Baby, you're already everything in this world. To us.*

END OF PLAY